A Tradition for Freedom

A Tradition for Freedom

The Story of
University College School

Nigel Watson

JAMES
X
JAMES

© University College School, 2007
First published 2007
ISBN 1 904022 05 7

Project Editor: Susan Millership
Design: Vimbai Shire
Archive photography: Robin Farrow
UCS Project Co-ordinator: Helen Sender

Printed and bound by Butler & Tanner Ltd
Frome,
United Kingdom

Published by James & James (Publishers) Ltd
Gordon House Business Centre
6 Lissenden Gardens
London NW5 1LX

Picture Acknowledgements

Many of the illustrations come from material in the
School archive and individual Old Scholars' collec-
tions and the publishers are grateful for permission
to reproduce pictures from the following:
BBC Photo Library 61; Leighton Museum 23;
Michael Diamond/ArenaPAL/TopFoto 24;
Museum of London/HIP/Topfoto 76; Print
Collector/HIP/TopFoto 10; Topham/Picturepoint
79; The Luis A. Ferre Foundation Inc., Ponce,
Puerto Rico / Christie's Images Ltd 23; Hampstead
Museum/Burgh House 72; Topham/Picturepoint 24.

Illustrations
JACKET, MAIN PICTURE: Bruno Roncarati (parent),
Mike Alsford (second left) and David Lund leading
one of the many Fun Runs organised by David
Lund for charity.
HALF TITLE: Boys on history field trip.
TITLE PAGE: Aerial view of the school at Frognal.
THIS PAGE: Front entrance.

Contents

Acknowledgements

UCS is a school with a distinctive tradition which has been sustained consistently from the foundation of the school to the present day. It has been fascinating tracing the way different generations have interpreted this tradition. Part of this tradition seems to be a self-effacing modesty about the school's history – the school has very little of the copious written material relating to the legion of many distinguished former pupils, and its archive is remarkably haphazard, with, for instance, a large part of the Council minutes simply having disappeared, and with material scattered over different parts of the school. So there were a few difficulties involved in putting this short history together. I could not have done without the help of Helen Sender, who made the task of tracking down information, arranging interviews and sorting out all the other bits and pieces involved in a project like this so much easier; nor without the advice and assistance of Rebecca Hemming, the school librarian, who helped me obtain material about the school and its pupils.

The main documentary sources included – a full run of the school magazine from 1869 onwards; an intermittent run of Council minutes from 1905 onwards; several volumes of collected press cuttings from around 1910 to the mid-1950s; several earlier histories; memoirs by former pupils and staff, including Stephen Spender, H C Barnard, Ivor Wilkinson, Richard Pike, Guy Kendall, Vivian de Sola Pinto, K R A Hart and Teddy Vogel; a collection of material at the National Archive, including inspection reports; and a collection of material relating to the early history of the school held at UCL Special Collections, including a run of headmaster's reports from 1842 to 1904.

But I am also greatly indebted to all those past and present staff and former pupils who spoke to me or wrote to me about their time at UCS. I would like to thank the current headmaster, Kenneth Durham, and Council chairman, Sir Victor Blank; and Mike Alsford, Geoff Brown, Geoffrey Carrick, John Couper, Tony Hillier, Colin Holloway, John Hubbard, Geoffrey Maitland Smith, Ian McGregor, Eric Marston, Aubrey Morley, Terry Morris, John Older, Richard Pike, John Slack, Giles Slaughter and Peter Underwood. Their contributions have made a vital difference.

Ultimate responsibility, however, lies with the author and even if my views of past personalities and events may not chime with those of every reader with experience of the school, I hope they provoke comment at least. In any case I believe there is no such thing as a definitive history and, in relation to a thriving institution like UCS, this must be seen as a work in progress. Charting the school's development thus far has been a most enjoyable task.

Nigel Watson
SPRING 2007

Foreword

We are delighted at UCS to have the opportunity of reviewing the School's historic achievements so close to the centenary of its move from Gower Street. The illustrations in this book show what an interesting and varied time it has been. I am equally pleased that it will now be possible to assess the remarkable progress of UCS on its Hampstead site.

Nigel Watson has reflected in an admirable way the ethos that we believe to be so important at UCS – of a liberal education founded firmly upon respectful and open relationships between students and their teachers, the emphasis upon individuality tempered by team-work, and ambition balanced by kindness.

UCS is committed to fostering independence of mind, together with a long-standing belief in tolerance and respect for the individual, and this commitment can be seen to have characterised the School's history.

A Tradition for Freedom describes the mould-breaking establishment of the 'Godless College' on Gower Street in 1830 by the group of radicals who opened high-quality education to those of any religious belief and none. It traces, from that beginning, the development of UCS in Hampstead and its emergence today as one of the finest and best-resourced schools in the UK.

It is an insightful retrospective for Old Gowers, pupils, parents and anyone with an interest in our remarkable school.

Kenneth Durham
HEADMASTER
SPRING 2007

1

'Without distinction of race, colour or creed'

1830–1880

University College School, or UCS as it is always known, is different from almost any other school. It was founded in 1830 with this deliberate intention. There was the whiff of revolution in the air. All the old certainties seemed under threat. Widespread economic distress revived pressure for parliamentary reform, which was coupled with attacks on the religious establishment. Concessions had to be made. The first was the repeal in 1828 of the Test and Corporation Acts in as far as they prevented Protestant nonconformists from holding public office. Among the politicians leading this assault was Lord John Russell, later to succeed Peel as prime minister. In the same year

The School playground in 1833, from an engraving by the artist George Scharf. Scharf's son, also called George, was a pupil at the School.

Key figures in the founding of University College, London.
ABOVE: Lord John Russell, politician.

BELOW: Henry Brougham, politician.

BOTTOM: Thomas Campbell, poet.

he was also one of the central figures involved in founding University College, London, along with Henry Brougham, soon to be Lord Chancellor in Grey's reforming government, and the poet Thomas Campbell.

The birth of University College, known until 1836 as the University of London, was utterly in keeping with the times. Oxford and Cambridge were totems of the Anglican establishment, whose degrees were closed to those unwilling to subscribe on oath to the Thirty-Nine Articles. The education they offered was in any case narrow and dominated by the classics. Those who supported Brougham, Russell and others, and espoused the cause of reform, wished to send their own sons to a college where, regardless of their faith, they would receive a broader education to prepare them for the professions.

The new college drew its inspiration, appropriately enough for a cosmopolitan institution, from diverse sources. Many of its supporters were children of the Enlightenment, characterised by intellectual toleration and a confidence in progress. Russell and Brougham, for instance, were students at Edinburgh University when the Scottish universities were the keystone of Scotland's Enlightenment. They were also aware of developments in the United States, where Jefferson, founding the University of Virginia in 1825, had scoured Europe to recruit scholars to teach a broad curriculum, including philosophy, law, modern languages, medicine, science and the arts.

British universities catered for an elite and this remained unchanged until the end of the twentieth century. Although the first students attending University College may have come from a broader social base than those at Oxford or Cambridge, they were privileged nevertheless. The College admitted young men over the age of fifteen, following a pattern set by the Scottish universities. With fewer students than anticipated, it was crucial to secure a constant supply, so it was unsurprising that Brougham and certain of his colleagues decided to open a school connected with the College. Once again, a key inspiration came from the Enlightenment, in this case Jeremy Bentham, the philosopher of utilitarianism, now in the twilight of his days. Bentham's dissatisfaction with his own religious and classically based education had spurred his thinking. His work on the subject, *Chrestomathia* (from 'chrestos' meaning useful and 'mathos' meaning knowledge or learning), contained a stinging attack on the schools fostered by the Church of England for their insistence that religion had a major role in the education of the poor. Bentham had a broad concept of a useful curriculum. His own list encompassed maths, physical science, modern languages, economics, law and music – a far cry from the staple diet of classics and religion in most schools.

Educational reform had barely begun in the 1820s. In the first half of the century, those boys – and they were almost all boys – privileged to receive something approximating a secondary education found it mainly in private schools in urban areas. Such a school was the one opened by Brougham and his friends. An announcement appeared in *The Times* on 29 September 1829, although the Council of University College only approved the idea in February 1830. While the school was entirely independent of the College, approval was vital if pupils were to progress from the school to the College. The intention was to open the school before the end of 1830. The search for a headmaster was one of some urgency.

Perhaps it was a mistake to accept a recommendation from an Anglican cleric, even if he was as enlightened in his views as Edward Maltby, later Bishop of Durham. Maltby's man, Henry Browne, was also a clergyman, as well as the son of a clergyman, and a scholar of Corpus Christi, Cambridge. Browne, a young man of twenty-six, may have shared his mentor's beliefs, but the prospectus he drew up betrayed the depth of his Anglican roots. Although it referred to 'a sound liberal education', Browne described the new school as a 'Classical Day School', with a staple diet of Latin, Greek, English and mathematics. There would be no science and school would open every day with 'a short exercise of devotion'. Browne made clear that it was possible to obtain an exemption from this assembly, but it was all too much for those who wanted the school to share the non-sectarian values of the College. Ironically, once the school was well established, it would again be influenced by the concept that the teaching of the classics remained the summit of any boy's education. At its most extreme, this would create a narrower curriculum for many boys. Religion too would return, by which time there would seem nothing controversial about the idea of 'a short exercise in devotion'.

A new prospectus was quickly issued, emphasising that a boy's religion would be the responsibility only of his parents or guardians. The school was also unusual in stating that 'school discipline will be conducted without recourse to corporal punishment'. Instead, other punishments, including impositions and detention, would be employed, although the prospectus continued: 'when advice, remonstrance, and censure fail, the subject cannot be considered a desirable companion for the other pupils and must be removed'.

On 1 November 1830 the London University School opened at 16 Lower Gower Street, with fifty-eight boys. Although numbers increased to 116 by the following February – a clear indication that the school was meeting a local need – Browne was never comfortable and soon resigned. His replacement was an assistant master, John Walker, a graduate of Trinity College, Dublin.

The original premises were already cramped and parents had been pressing the Council of University College to admit the school 'within the walls' of the College. The school remained entirely separate from the College, however, despite the fact that several of the school's founding

Jeremy Bentham is often credited with being the founder of University College, London although he was 80 years old when the University opened in 1828, and took no part in its establishment. He still deserves to be considered as its spiritual father as he supported education for all, regardless of race, creed or political belief: the founding tenets of both the University and the School. Bentham's preserved skeleton, dressed in his own clothes, and surmounted by a wax head was moved to UCL in 1850 and remains there to this day.

George Cruikshank's cartoon of Henry Brougham hawking shares in the University around Lincoln's Inn, 1825.

THE LONDON UNIVERSITY SCHOOL,

16, Lower Gower-street, Bedford-square (Head Master the Rev. Henry Browne, M.A. of Corpus Christi College, Cambridge), will Open on the 1st of November.

This Institution is a Classical Day School, including those branches of a liberal education usually taught to boys from about eight to fifteen years of age.

The subjects of instruction are—

I. The Latin and Greek Languages.

II. The English, French, and German Languages.

III. Outlines of History and Geography.

IV. Writing, Ciphering, and (if desired) Pencil Drawing and the Principles of Perspective.

Terms 15l. per annum, payable by instalments, and no extra charges —the pupils providing books.

Hours of attendance from nine to twelve in the morning; two to four in the afternoon. For Pupils residing at a distance, in whose case a different arrangement may be desirable, the attendance will be from nine to three, including one hour for recreation.

Copies of the Prospectus may be had at the School; at the Office of the London University; and of the following Booksellers:—

Taylor, Upper Gower-street	Templeman, Percy-street
Nimmo, ditto	Treuttel and Co., Soho-square
Lloyd, Harley-street	Alexander, Great Russell-street
Gardener, Regent-street	Crew and Spencer, Lamb's Con-
Murray, Albemarle-street	duit-street
Knight, Pall-mall East	Fellows, Ludgate-street
Wyld, Charing-cross	Jenny and Chaplin, Cheapside
Smith, Strand	Richardson, Cornhill
Underwood, Fleet-street	Parbury and Co., Leadenhall-st.

The Head Master may be spoken with at the School daily (except Sundays), between the hours of 11 and 4.

Such pupils as are already entered are requested to take an early opportunity of calling upon the Head Master, that they may be examined and classed accordingly.

HENRY BROWNE, Head Master.

An early advertisement for the School, 1830.

subscribers were members of Council. A majority of Council had also been opposed to 'any intimate connexion with the school', as one early document put it, probably because it was regarded as a low priority and a hindrance to other developments within the College. Parental pressure finally prevailed though, and in October 1831 the Council agreed to take over the school, which moved in January 1832 to occupy the College's great hall and the rooms immediately below it. Despite this adoption, the College remained ambivalent towards the school, to the detriment of its development over the next seventy-five years. When the College changed its name in 1836, so too did the school, becoming the Junior School of University College, and then University College School (or UCS) two years later.

Before the move took place, the sudden departure of the second headmaster within a year further disrupted the early life of UCS. Walker knew that he was a stand-in who would not automatically remain headmaster when the College took over the school. His chances of doing so vanished altogether when it transpired that he had been declared bankrupt in 1825 and was still in debt.

It was hardly surprising that all this upheaval reduced the school's roll to

13

Thomas Hewitt Key, professor of Latin and headmaster of the School from 1831 to 1875. He was known for his friendliness and sent out monthly reports to parents.

Henry Malden, professor of Greek and joint headmaster of the School with Key from 1831 to 1842.

eighty by Easter 1832. The decline was a temporary one. Council placed the school's fortunes in the hands of two young men. When Thomas Hewitt Key and his colleague Henry Malden agreed in December 1831 to take over the school as joint headmasters at their own risk, they began a tradition of youthful heads at UCS. Key was thirty-three and Malden thirty-two. They were also the first in a line of classically educated heads, whose professed aim was to move away from the classical straitjacket in which most schools had become constrained.

They were remarkable men. In 1825 Key was the founding professor of pure mathematics at Jefferson's University of Virginia, counting Edgar Allan Poe among his pupils. After his return to England, Key became the first professor in Roman language, literature and antiquities at the new London University, and retained this post until he became sole headmaster of UCS in 1842. In his younger years he was tall and impressive, genial and handsome; his later increase in girth earned him the nickname 'Tub', although this, together with his sweeping mane of white hair, only added to the physical impression he made on the boys.

Key was later referred to as the Red Queen to the White Queen of his shyer and gentler companion. Henry Malden was an outstanding scholar at Trinity College, Cambridge, where he was bracketed with the famous Whig historian, Thomas Macaulay, a lifelong friend, in the scholarship examinations. When he became joint headmaster he also took up the chair in Greek at the College, which he retained until his resignation shortly before he died in 1876, a year after the death of Key. Although Malden gave up his school post in 1842, he continued to teach Greek to senior boys until 1868.

Key and Malden, like the school's founders, were influenced by the ideas of the Enlightenment. Their influence permeated the school so deeply that it still survives today. Under their charge, it was the teaching that mattered; everything else was almost incidental. They brought pupils and staff closer together than was usual in almost any other school, creating an atmosphere of mutual respect which UCS has never lost. As Key pointed out to Council:

> it has been my constant practice to cultivate a sort of personal acquaintance with the boys and to invite them to make confidential communications to me; and I doubt whether there is any large school in the country where the headmaster is so ready to hear the complaints of the boys as regards their schoolfellows or their masters, as in ours.

Neither man kept their pupils at arm's length. Key was a lively teacher who often chalked up problems on the blackboard and invited his pupils to come to the front of the class to solve them. He treated his senior boys never as pupils,

DISCIPLINE, AND GENERAL MANAGEMENT

Discipline is maintained without corporal punishment or written impositions.

The BLACK BOOK is a record of offences against discipline and is submitted to the Committee of Management. Duplicates of entries are sent to the parents of the boys concerned.

For minor offences a boy's name is entered in the APPEARING BOOK, and parents are notified at the discretion of the Head Master.

Boys who are late, or whose home work is defective, are entered in the TASK BOOK, and are detained out of school-hours to discharge arrears. The period of detention does not exceed one hour.

Boys whose class-work is unsatisfactory may be detained by the Class Master for a period not exceeding one hour.

When a boy is reported as persistently idle, or when it is desired to obtain an exact account of a boy's work at any particular time, his name is placed ON REPORT TO THE HEAD MASTER. Such boys present weekly, on Fridays, a printed Form to all the Masters who teach them, and obtain a written report from each. This Form must be shown by the boy the same afternoon to the Head Master, by whom it is initialled and given back to him to be signed by his Father or Guardian. The shortest time for which a boy is put On Report is four weeks.

The discipline of the School is maintained out of School hours, so far as it is possible, by the Monitors. Half of the Monitors are appointed by the Head Master and half elected by the Monitorial body, subject to the general approval of the Staff.

Boys are expected to settle their differences and adjust their relations, so far as is possible, without the intervention of Masters. Any boy who has a grievance should apply, in the first instance, to the School Captain or a Monitor; or he may ask his parents (or guardian) to communicate with the Head Master. All such communications are treated as confidential.

The School rejected corporal punishment from the start, preferring to rely on the 'Black Book', 'Task Book' and the 'Appearing Book' to maintain discipline.

but as students. Key and Malden were also responsible for UCS's much more relaxed approach to discipline. The disregard they had for what went on outside the classroom occasionally got them into trouble. It was only when a beadle by the name of Watson was employed in the 1840s that misbehaviour within the school, and particularly within the playground, began to decline. From Malden comes another surviving characteristic of the school. It was said of him that he did not place 'as much stress on outward observances, if only he thought his boys were really interested in the spirit of their lesson'.

Discipline was based on a punishment book, recording serious offences, and known from its binding as the Black Book, and the self-explanatory Task

Book. Key later added what was called the Appearance or Appearing Book, bound in white vellum, listing those boys whose offences demanded an appearance before the head. Key never employed corporal punishment and only rarely resorted to other penalties. Such penalties, however, could be both eccentric and cruel. One boy chastised for lying was made to stand on a form-bench, wearing his jacket inside out. Another, who had been thieving, was strapped to the staircase banisters during playtime, as an example. A common punishment was being locked up for several hours in the small confinement room. And although his preference was for a relaxed and tolerant regime, the head also had the strength of character to assert his authority when necessary.

Speech Day, 1848, drawn by Thomas Hood for the first UCS magazine called *Miscellany*. Hood later became the editor of children's annuals.

This was strikingly illustrated during the so-called great lock-out, when the boys barricaded themselves into the Long Room all day. As the doors were forced, they showered the advancing party of beadles and masters with well-aimed pieces of coal and pebbles from behind upturned furniture. But Key appeared at the opposite end of the room, having taken a disused staircase, and at the height of the fight his loud and familiar voice rang out, ordering every boy to stand with his face to the wall. The riot was over.

It has been argued that the influence of Key and Malden over such a long period – Key remained in office until 1875 – combined with the distinctive nature of UCS to prevent it from taking advantage of the educational developments that later gushed forth. Quite clearly, however, this isolation from external developments had been an advantage for the school when it was founded. There is no doubt that the two men made an indelible imprint on the school.

Malden and Key found it impossible to keep two jobs going at the same time. After more than a decade, Malden chose to return to full-time academic work while Key remained as sole headmaster. But for several years afterwards Malden carried out an annual assessment of the teaching and work done in the school. This was innovative for the time. Key himself often sat in classes to observe how masters taught and controlled the boys. He was also unusual in taking soundings from parents with whom he was friendly and, through the monthly reports sent out to all parents, inviting them to come and see him if they had anything to discuss. From the 1850s he also met weekly with his staff. All this allowed Key to monitor standards of teaching. If staff were unsuitable, he rarely hesitated in dismissing them. But he was a fair man. No master was ever dismissed or asked to resign until a full investigation had taken place and he had been given a chance to refute any allegations. Key was also a man with a sense of proportion. He knew that the relaxed atmosphere at the school – it was considered odd that mortar boards were never worn by staff – sometimes seemed anarchic to outside observers. He defended staff against unfounded criticism and would never let minor faults cloud his judgement of a master's quality of teaching. Crucially, he allowed them considerable freedom within the curriculum. One former pupil, the eminent proponent of technical education, Sir Philip Magnus, the first director of the City & Guilds Institute, later recalled that the high standard of education he received at UCS in the 1850s 'was largely the result of the freedom enjoyed by the teachers, and to the close attention they gave to the needs and requirements of their pupils'.

It was fitting that the eccentric but talented band of staff Key and Malden gathered around them reflected the cosmopolitan nature of the school. In the 1850s these included Professor Merlet, the French master, with his auburn wig, Mr Newnham Travers with his cork leg, and the drawing master, Monsieur Polszcywytschi, known as 'Ploz', reputed to be an impoverished

A drawing of boys using the outside 'gymnasium' in 1845.

refugee Polish count. Travers, who taught Latin, English and almost anything else on request, was typical of many of his colleagues during this period, who were often asked to teach a little bit of everything.

UCS seemed to specialise in employing liberal Frenchmen with a political conscience. Monsieur Cassal, who taught languages from 1856 to 1885, had been prominent in the 1848 Revolution and a member of the Constituent Assembly. After the 1851 coup d'état, he fled to Britain after escaping being hanged from a lamp post when the rope gave way. One of his colleagues, Monsieur Bocquet, failed to turn up at the beginning of the autumn term in 1870. The cause was the Franco-Prussian War. It turned out, as the headmaster reported, that 'in his distress at the tremendous reverses of the French armies he was carried away by an irresistible impulse to abandon at once all his appointments for the purpose of offering his services, whatever they might be worth, to the then French government'. Bocquet's offer, even though he was past fifty, was accepted; he became the commandant of a National Guard battalion in Paris, and after several adventures eventually returned to London, where he was taken back at UCS.

From the early 1830s to the 1850s the number of boys remained around 250. There were times when the school found it hard to keep up the numbers. Drawing its boys from middle-class parents in trade and the professions, UCS was affected by periodic downturns in the economy. There was growing competition from other schools, several of them learning from UCS to their advantage. In 1845 Key noted how the head of the City of London School, although an Anglican clergyman, played down the Anglican aspects of the school to attract boys from the same clientele as UCS. In the mid-1850s numbers started to increase once more, exceeding 300 and rising steadily towards 400. Another boost came in 1870–71, when the Franco-Prussian War led many boys to come to UCS rather than being educated abroad. By the time of Key's retirement there were 589 boys at the school.

The boys were a cosmopolitan bunch. This too has been a constant characteristic of the school. The non-sectarian ethos and the breadth of the curriculum, wrote one former pupil, attracted 'boys from almost every country, tongue and rank on the earth, from wherever indeed education was not liberal or unfettered'. Parents of such a boy were attracted by Key's belief, as he once advised parents, that to follow

a liberal profession, it is absolutely necessary in order that he may manfully succeed to his own satisfaction, that he shall be able to clear away all prejudice, and to gauge and weigh the men he meets by their own individual merit, whatever their parentage may be and whatever their set may be.

Earnest Goddard, a pupil at Gower Street.

By the late 1850s there were many boys of foreign birth or descent at the school. The list of names included Varicas, van Sandan, Arroyo, Corinaldi, Breda, Monte, Scharfenberg, Faija and Calogera. There were several Parsees, including Naorajee Pohcha, Framjee Bomanjee Cama and Ardesir Cursetjee. Among the sons of political refugees were the brothers Pulszky (Hungary), Blind and Kinkel (Germany). Jewish boys too were an important part of the school from the very beginning. Among the earliest pupils was Moses Angel, later the founder of the *Jewish Chronicle*. Hermann Adler, who was to become a controversial chief rabbi, attended the school in the 1850s. Adler would later recall that it was the warm welcome he and fellow immigrant Jews received from Key at UCS that led them to love their adopted country. One of Alder's contemporaries at UCS was another notable boy of Jewish descent, Alfred Yarrow, one of the Victorian era's outstanding marine engineers and shipbuilders, and the founder of the great firm on the Clyde which bore his name. Yarrow remembered the special relationship between boys and staff and among the boys themselves. The maths master, Cook, discovering that Yarrow and his best friend, Rutt, had fallen out, made sure the two boys shook

Five Japanese students at University College in 1863. They were among the first Japanese to study in the West and they were followed by a number of boys who enrolled in the School.

hands, forgave and forgot, and resumed their friendship. This lasted a lifetime, even though they found themselves at opposite ends of the world.

In the 1860s the first of a stream of Japanese boys came to UCS on the advice of the Foreign Secretary, the Earl of Derby. They came to study in England as part of the conscious process of opening Japan to Western influence for the first time. After returning to their native country, several of them later took up important public positions, one of them, Hayashi, returning to the UK as the Japanese Ambassador. He too echoed the judgement of other former pupils about UCS, that more than any other school it had 'thrown open its gates and afforded its advantages without distinction of race, colour or creed'.

For a time, alongside the sons of poor immigrants and distinguished foreigners, the school also hosted a handful of boarders, the sons of nonconformist families whose wealth came from the mills and factories of Yorkshire and Lancashire. As Alfred Yarrow later noted, they 'had not to trouble much about making a place for themselves in the world'. They lodged in private houses, often with members of staff. In the 1920s there were still a dozen or so boarders at the school.

Rising numbers created several problems for Key. The pressing need for more accommodation was solved when the school moved into the new south wing of University College, constructed in three phases between 1860 and 1876. A more pressing difficulty was the school's inability to employ enough staff. UCS, founded without any endowments and reliant on fees, was understaffed and could scarcely afford new appointments, let alone decent salaries for existing staff, who, for lack of any pension arrangements, often stayed on long after they should have retired. This turned out to be a problem that persisted well into the twentieth century.

Key must have been grateful for the support he received from Robert Horton, who joined the staff as a young man in 1857. Horton, a classics scholar from Peterhouse, Cambridge, would prove an outstanding lieutenant

The new south wing brought welcome extra space for the School.

A view of the College showing the new south wing (far right) constructed for the School between 1860 and 1876.

ABOVE LEFT: The headmaster's room in the south wing.

RIGHT: The monitors' room in the south wing.

Temple Orme attended the School in the 1850s and was a master from 1868 to 1910. He was the School's first archivist.

for Key. With so few staff and so many of them so old, Horton, like Key, knew how important it was for the school to maintain a close rapport with the boys. As one master, Temple Orme, later reflected, this was a time when 'the boys constituted a sort of republic – it may have been a turbulent republic'. As Key aged, Horton assumed more of his responsibilities, taking up the position of vice-master in 1866. In the June 1884 edition of the school magazine it was said that he had a 'power of getting at boys' and influencing them, as well as a way of 'encouraging confidence which made the most nervous and timid willing to unbosom himself of his difficulties'. Horton was held in great respect and there was apparently only one instance of a boy attempting to take advantage of him. A well-built boy had been causing a rumpus near Horton's room and tried to push past him. Horton turned pale, and the next moment, much to the surprise of those who did not suspect Horton of physical strength, the boy 'found himself quietly dropped on the floor'. Horton was nicknamed 'Pup', due to his youthful appearance, but overwork wore him out and he died in 1884, aged just forty-eight.

In some respects this was a golden era for UCS, despite the fact that the school was hampered, first, by the poor teaching that many new boys had received at their previous schools, and second, because none of the boys stayed on after the age of sixteen. Key sought to tackle the first problem, which consumed much of his staff's time, through the junior school he persuaded Council to set up in 1862. UCS could only benefit if boys came to the school after receiving an education along UCS lines at the junior school. The school lasted eleven years before closing in May 1873. It was not for lack of success. It closed because Council needed to save money after spending significant sums on College improvements. The idea, however, would be resurrected a generation later.

An early leaving age did not prevent many boys either from finding their way to Oxbridge or achieving prominence in their chosen fields. This says much for the school, but also gives an indication of the calibre of the boys whose parents were attracted by the school. One striking characteristic is how many talented scientists and mathematicians UCS turned out during this period, which must say something about the strength of science teaching at the school – again, something not found in many schools at the time. A string of former pupils, from Edward Routh in the 1840s to Percy Frankland in the 1870s, became fellows of the Royal Society.

UCS boys did not excel only in academic spheres. UCS produced a remarkable number of outstanding politicians, including Joseph Chamberlain, John Morley and Rufus Isaacs. In 1906 nineteen former pupils were returned as Members of Parliament. Illustrious former pupils in the world of the arts ranged from Frederic Leighton, the prominent painter and the first artist to be ennobled, and Richard D'Oyly Carte, the impresario forever associated with Gilbert and Sullivan, to Hamo Thornycroft, one of the outstanding sculptors of his time. Several outstanding industrialists and professional men also attended the school, including Sir Henry Doulton, the founder of Doulton pottery, in the 1830s, and Edwin Waterhouse, founder of the accountancy

University College School produced many outstanding politicians including Joseph Chamberlain who entered the House of Commons as a Liberal candidate for Birmingham in 1876. In the election of 1906 nineteen former pupils were returned as Members of Parliament.

Frederic Leighton was a hugely successful Victorian painter. He became the first English artist to be given a peerage. *Flaming June* (BELOW LEFT) was painted in 1895.

23

Richard D'Oyly Carte produced the operas of Gilbert and Sullivan. He founded the D'Oyly Carte Opera Company in 1876 and opened the Savoy Theatre a few years later.

Iolanthe programme from the Savoy.

practice that bears his name, in the 1850s. All this glittering talent justified the remark made by one writer in the school magazine in 1869:

> if there is anything which more than another distinguishes this school, except indeed the liberality with which it opens its doors to all, without regard to religious creeds, it is the varied range of subjects taught, which enables those who have the requisite natural abilities to become statesmen, philosophers or poets.

Many boys found their craving for knowledge satisfied by the broad curriculum devised and sustained by Key and Malden, and delivered by a group of often talented teachers. By the 1840s the subjects covered included Latin and Greek, French and German, English, history and geography, mathematics, chemistry and physics. The school's strength in science, illustrated by the roll call of illustrious former pupils, benefited from teaching given in the school by professors from the College, including the professor of chemistry, Alexander Williamson, and the professor of physics, Carey Foster. By 1870, when a government enquiry discovered only thirteen schools with a science laboratory, UCS was adding two more to the original laboratory created in 1858. The weakness in the school's science teaching was that it was confined largely to senior boys.

Under Key's influence, the classics retained a central place in the curriculum, although he sometimes had to fight the feeling among some parents attracted by the school that Greek and Latin were, as he recorded, of 'little practical utility'. He was less enthusiastic about the humanities, believing history to be almost a waste of time in school; the subject was among the less distinguished at UCS for several generations. But the school was innovative in other areas. Remarkably for the times, by the 1870s boys were learning Spanish and Italian, in addition to French and German, while Euclid had given way to geometry in the teaching of mathematics.

Another unusual feature of the school was the pupil-centred nature of the curriculum, derived from Bentham's chrestomathic principles. This was very much in tune with Key's belief in taking a personal interest in each boy. Every subject was optional, although most boys intending to proceed to University College took the Greek, Latin and mathematics required for entrance. Philip Magnus remembered that all new boys in 1854 were examined over several days to assess their ability and establish what they wanted to study. Each boy was then given his own individual timetable and allotted to different groups for each preferred subject, according to his ability. Apparently there were 250 possible combinations. To cater for the varying academic progress of each boy in every subject, school examinations were held three times a year, in addition to the London Matriculation examinations. The whole system, in

Many of the teachers at the School in the 19th century also held positions at the University. LEFT: Carey Foster, Professor of physics.

BELOW: Alexander Williamson, Professor of chemistry.

fact, was partly geared towards the demands of the London Matriculation required for entrance into the College, which became something of a hindrance later on as opportunities expanded for higher education elsewhere.

As noted earlier, this splendid isolation was also a virtue. Any criticism of the curriculum for being oriented too much towards examinations – one that might be made with equal validity today – should not obscure the fact that UCS was still streets ahead of other schools in many respects. Magnus recorded how Key realised that many boys would leave school for commerce, industry and the professions. He believed that they should have some knowledge of 'the duties of citizenship, of the relations, even then troubled, between capital and labour, and of the conditions of the production and distribution of wealth'. A speaker was invited to give several lectures on the subject, 'then known as social science', to selected boys. And UCS was not totally unaware of external developments or internal weaknesses. Horton, for instance, was advocating reform of UCS's curricular organisation in 1870.

As the school filled up, it became clear that the boys needed something other than rioting to keep them occupied outside the classroom. Sporting activities were somewhat haphazard because of the lack of suitable playing fields, but cricket and fives were played. In the 1860s an athletic sports association was started, a rowing club was briefly established and rugby was introduced, most matches appearing to have taken place at Primrose Hill. All

the boys had been instructed in gym since at least the 1840s and also had the opportunity of taking fencing lessons. After an abortive attempt in the 1850s, a cadet corps was established in 1871 as the 'B' (later 'D') Company of the London Rifle Brigade. Other activities relied on the initiative of the boys and were limited largely to debates, games of chess and the very occasional concert. The school debating society had been founded by Philip Magnus in 1857, before which boys had held debates in their own homes.

Nevertheless, by the 1870s, all this was fairly limited by comparison with many of the new public schools and some of the reformed grammar schools. Despite Horton's advocacy, the unwieldy organisation of the curriculum had still not been reformed, and it was clear that in a school of more than 500 boys other areas of school management required revision. Key also realised that more boys created the need for more and better-paid staff in improved accommodation, neither of which Council was prepared to accept. Instead, Key spent a lot of his time attempting to resist Council's attempts to make financial economies.

Officers' Training Camp, 1912. The School's first cadet corps was established in 1871.

Memorial

to the

Council of University College

from

Former Pupils of the School

in favour of the election of

Mr E. R. Horton M.A.

as

Head Master of the School

March 1876

The title page of a testimonial in support of Elias Robert Horton's candidacy for the post of headmaster. It was signed by over 600 former pupils but this was not enough to sway the School Council in his favour. In *An Angel Without Wings*, an early history of UCS, the author remarks on this decision, 'The Council ... in one of the most extraordinary appointments since Caligula made his horse a consul.'

Key died in office in 1875. His successor was Henry Weston Eve. In his mid-thirties, well-built, athletic, sociable and hospitable, Eve had been educated at Mill Hill, Rugby and Trinity College, Cambridge. He was reputedly, and appropriately for UCS, an agnostic. Although he was a classicist, his teaching career had been spent developing the modern side of the curriculum at Wellington College, one of the new public schools, founded as a boarding school in 1853 in memory of the Duke of Wellington. Eve was easily imitated, with his habit of fiddling with his watch chain and a distinctive drawl ('Some vulgah little beggah-ah has been scwibbling on the lockahs. Ah-if detected-ah he will be dealt with most severelah'). He was a good teacher, but could seem aloof, which did nothing to win him over to a school massively disappointed that the popular Horton, who had been acting head during Key's last illness, had been passed over. Eve's first prizegiving was marred by the boys shouting out: 'Three cheers for Mr Horton!'

2

'A mere department of something else'

1880–1907

Eve was ambitious for the school, but his ambitions, as well as those of his two successors, were severely curtailed by two factors: the school remained short of money and its development was hindered by the dithering surrounding the eventual removal of UCS from Gower Street. Eve's annual reports to Council are peppered with the phrase, 'a great Public School', in reference to UCS, as if he believed that simply repeating the words would help his aspirations come true. Heavily influenced by his time at Wellington College, he also appreciated and valued the non-sectarian nature of the school – few schools at the time offered the opportunity for anyone other than a clergyman to become head.

The opening of University College School in Frognal by King Edward VII, accompanied by Queen Alexandra and their daughter, Princess Victoria, 1907.

Henry Weston Eve, headmaster 1876–1898.

This, he believed, accounted for UCS's distinctive 'sweet reasonableness'. Although he must have found the form system at UCS distinctly eccentric, he always upheld the principle, as he once told a gathering of old boys, of 'giving every boy an opportunity of rising high in the school in the subjects for which he was most apt'. While he wished to raise intellectual standards as far as possible, he was also certain that at UCS 'it is above all the education that boys give one another that tells most on their future life. It is in their intercourse with one another that they learn those lessons that are most valuable afterwards'. In this respect he was a fitting heir to the tradition forged by Key.

Eve quickly identified the weakness in the UCS form system. While it was supposed to be tailored to the individual needs of each boy, it nevertheless failed to create strong links between pupils and any one master, since no boy was ever a constant member of one form. Eve soon introduced the system of consulting masters, each taking responsibility for a group, known as a Consult, of approximately fifty boys. Eve reported to Council in 1876–77 that the change was well received, commenting that 'the personal influence of the Consulting Master on his boys is the main object I have desired to secure'.

Eve retained the school's chrestomathic scheme. It was never satisfactory. One new boy, H.C. Barnard, joining UCS in 1897, found himself in U2 for French, L3 for maths, U3 for arithmetic, L4 for Greek, English, history and geography, and U4 for Latin. Eve wanted to teach an expanded range of science subjects much earlier in a boy's school career, rather than linking science specifically to the London Matriculation. Certainly elementary science classes were introduced within his first year, but Barnard, who specialised in classics, recalled that he never had a single science lesson. The conflict between classics and science teaching would remain a running theme in the history of the school's curricular development until the 1950s.

It may be that the curricular changes Eve wished to make were hindered by his inability either to replace existing staff or to recruit new staff members. He complained to Council as soon as he arrived that his staff were badly paid. He managed to improve the salaries of the lowest paid (which still remained almost half the minimum being paid at Rugby, for instance), but was unable to do much more, despite sacrificing part of his own income for later increases. Council, which never consulted the headmaster on financial matters, rarely reviewed salaries, even though Eve pointed out that poorly paid masters were unable to move on, could not afford to give up and were difficult to replace. Eve calculated that during the first ten years of his headship the Council had transferred £15,000 (equivalent to well over a million pounds today) of the school's income to the College. It is hardly surprising that he complained about the lack of consultation or that he pressed for the school to become financially independent of the College.

Another characteristic of the school's history was the tendency for some heads to allow discipline to become too relaxed towards the end of their tenure. This happened under Key. One of the benefits of Eve's Consults was that they helped to improve discipline, partly by creating for the first time an organised structure for the boys. In addition, he worked through senior boys who had entered the school on his arrival and knew nothing of the lax times that had developed latterly under Key. Eve, somewhat obsessed with the public school system, was keen to develop an *esprit de corps* within UCS. He revived the ailing cadet corps, which he saw as 'an important element in the development of public spirit in the school'. In pursuit of this he also started a club for poor boys. 'The School ought,' he wrote, 'like other great Public Schools, to be associated with some kind of charitable work, of course absolutely unsectarian'. The club was opened on 1 January 1887 in a room at 45 Old Compton Street, moving later in the same year to a house in Wilmington Square in Clerkenwell. Helping out in the club was an eye-opener for the middle-class boys of UCS – there was a cultural gulf to be bridged.

UCS pupils and master, 1900.

Eve also fostered structured recreation through more school societies, including the science society, musical society and photographic society. Their popularity depended on the interest of the boys and how far they had to travel home after school. This also impeded Eve's ambitions for properly organised sporting activities. The school was still without a playing field when Eve took over. Out of his own pocket he secured pitches at Tufnell Park, but the access was unsatisfactory – it was through a pub. In 1884 he leased a field at Willesden Green, taken over by Council in 1886. Willesden was much more suitable, Eve told Council, since it provided the 'privacy and dignity befitting a great Public School'. Unfortunately it was still a long way from Gower Street and from the homes of many of the boys. School matches were played at Willesden until the move to a new ground at Neasden in 1900, although, given voluntary participation, the standard of team sports was never high. But cricket and rugby matches were played against neighbouring schools and the first match against an MCC side was played in 1891. If they wished, boys could also take part in

Rugby team, 1900.

swimming, tennis or cycling. A purpose-built gymnasium was opened in 1880. A Games Club, an umbrella society for all sports, was formed to encourage more boys to take part, but there was little improvement until Eve introduced house matches in 1885, for a shield awarded annually.

The houses, instead of being formed from the Consults, were based on form rooms, despite the obvious disadvantage this had in terms of inequality of age, and took their names from the Greek letters given to each form. In fact, it is uncertain that the Consults survived beyond the creation of the form-based houses. That is the implication of the recollection of one former pupil of the time, Leslie Wood, recorded in the school magazine at a later date. If that is the case, it is curious that Eve should have preferred the forms to the Consults as the basis for houses, since the retention of the chrestomathic system, with the dispersion of most boys to different forms for each subject, meant little form solidarity.

None of this could overcome the biggest problem facing Eve, which affected not just games, but every aspect of the school. Although numbers at the school continued to rise during the first few years of his headship, they peaked at 700 in 1879. Every year thereafter numbers fell, and there seemed nothing Eve could do about it. This had a serious impact on his plan to refresh the staff with new appointments at higher salaries, since this depended on raising more money through higher fees charged for an increasing number of pupils.

By the late nineteenth century many schools established in the heart of the capital found that conditions were becoming more and more unsatisfactory. Grime, crowds, traffic, stench, the threat to health in an age of high child mortality – all these were factors which made many schools consider whether or not to stay in London. Dulwich transferred to a greener site in 1870 and numbers quadrupled in eight years. Charterhouse moved out of London altogether in 1872, trebling the school roll. The City of London School took over new and larger premises on the Embankment in 1883 and St Paul's relocated to the suburb of West Kensington in 1884. Christ's Hospital first considered leaving the capital in the 1860s, but only made up its mind to move to rural Sussex in 1902. UCS was faced with the same quandary and took almost as long as Christ's Hospital to decide to do something about it.

By 1887 numbers at UCS had fallen to 500. Eve listed for Council the reasons for the decline: competition from more London day schools and provincial boarding schools; the movement of families to the suburbs; and ineffective financial management through the school's dependence on University College. He noted how the school's catchment area had shifted during the 1880s, with fewer boys from Bloomsbury, Bayswater, Notting Hill, Kensington, Regent's Park, Primrose Hill, Camden, Kentish Town and Islington, and more coming in from Belsize Park, Hampstead, Maida Vale, St

First XI, 1904.

Sporting success: Percy Furnivall won the title of Champion Bicyclist of the World in 1885. He attended the school from 1878 to 1883.

Charles Simmons, headmaster of Junior School, 1891–1919.

John's Wood and Kilburn. He had already raised the idea of moving out of central London, but Council would never do anything about it.

The suburb he had in mind was Hampstead. Here in 1891 he refounded the junior school. This was part of his attempt to recruit younger boys to UCS. Too many boys were being admitted to UCS at fourteen who only stayed for two years. This had an unsettling effect on the school. Fees were reduced to try to recruit more boys at an earlier age, but this, of course, did nothing to help the problems caused by lack of finance.

The Junior Branch (or JB as it became known) was opened at Holly Hill in Hampstead on 22 September 1891. The property was leased from Miss Ann Norton, who had previously run a girls' boarding house. To run the school, Eve transferred Charles Simmons from the staff at UCS, where he had been a member of the common room since 1880. Starting with twelve boys, the school had fifty-four pupils by Christmas. In the best traditions of UCS, Simmons deliberately established a broad curriculum, designed to prevent young boys from becoming bored. Natural history under Constance Garlick became a central part of Holly Hill's education, through the garden tended at the school and expeditions to the nearby Heath; and the school's four houses took the names of flowers – Iris, Marigold, Rose and Tulip.

Nevertheless, Eve was still running a school with fewer boys of a narrower age range. They were, he told Council, a happy band who worked hard, but the school was finding it difficult to attract able boys who might stay on after the age of sixteen. Eve did as much as he could to maintain standards. External examiners invited to the school in 1881 rated both mathematics and classics, the stepping stone to Oxbridge scholarships, highly satisfactory. Most boys presented for the London Matriculation passed the examination. And, despite Eve's problems, UCS was still producing a stream of boys from varied backgrounds who became renowned in their own fields and went on to make a difference in the world.

In ten years the roll at UCS fell from 500 in 1887 to 350 in 1897 with many boys staying only briefly. Most of the staff, still teaching a wide range of subjects across the curriculum, had been at the school before Eve became head. Their teaching methods were unchanged and many of them had lost any enthusiasm for their subjects. There were exceptions. One who typified the UCS tradition was John Russell, appointed in 1886. When he left to become head of a school in Hampstead, the boys recorded:

> we all knew he was a Socialist, that he believed in Ruskin, and didn't believe in wearing black ties or top hats. We shouldn't have been a bit surprised if he had turned up one fine summer morning wearing sandals. We sometimes used to speak of him jokingly as an Anarchist.

Paton's nonconformist background shone through the way he lived his life. His enthusiasm for fresh air stretched from cross-country runs and cycling to early-morning bathing parties and sleeping in a tent in his garden throughout the summer. He did not drink, smoke or gamble. He detested impropriety, insincerity and idleness, and never asked of anyone something he would not do himself. When he organised working parties of boys to paint the iron supports around the playing field so that they would appreciate the value of manual labour, Paton joined in himself. He cared little for how he dressed. When frock coat, silk hat and gloves were de rigueur for an evening appointment, Paton turned up in a tattered blazer. He cycled to school each morning in a combination of morning coat and plus fours, his frock trousers in a brown-paper parcel tied to the rear of the cycle.

His disregard for convention, his democratic instincts and impatience for change irritated some and antagonised others. But the boys were dazed and dazzled by him. He was interested in the boys for themselves, each as an individual, regardless of their ability. It was through the boys, his so-called Patonidae, the sons of Paton, that Paton exercised his greatest influence. He knew the name and seemed to have an inherent understanding of every boy. When he left, they paid him a warm tribute in the school magazine: 'He called us by our first names, knew most fellows better than their own consulting masters knew them… he found time to visit the stay-at-home, talk to the parent, coach the exam ridden, and help a hundred lame boys over innumerable stiles'. Paton's personal example was instrumental in allowing him to reinvigorate the school. In 1901 he was able to write 'that in few schools of the same size are discipline so smooth, the need of petty punishments so small, and the relations between master and pupil so cordial'.

It was unsurprising that Paton, as a convinced Christian, should introduce optional religious instruction to the school. Religion was no longer as contentious an issue as it had been when the school was founded and Paton saw no reason why boys who wished to learn about their faith should be denied the opportunity to do so. Nor was it surprising that the headmaster, with his enthusiasm for fresh air and physical activity, in the mould of many other muscular Christian heads of the time, should encourage improved sporting standards. In 1900 the unsuitable fields at Willesden were replaced, partly through funds raised in tribute to Paton's predecessor, with a playing field at Neasden. The rowing club was revived, over the Hammersmith to Putney course, and one UCS rower, Gordon Thomson, went on to win the gold medal in the coxless pairs in the 1908 London Olympics. Paton also fostered extra-curricular activities, including lectures by prominent visitors on a broad range of topics, from ancient Egypt to Britain's imperial naval ambitions.

John Lewis Paton became headmaster in 1899.

Paton faced the same problems as Eve. He stemmed the decline in numbers, which hovered around 350. He also admitted scholarship boys, supported by London County Council (LCC), for the first time in 1899. They joined the Commercial Department within the school, which had its beginnings under Eve. A number of schools carried out this experiment, providing instruction for a commercial education in return for a share of the grants now available to secondary schools from local authorities. At UCS, although the money was welcome, it was not a happy experience. Paton himself wrote that the boys were 'of good intellect and form excellent material for the Commercial Department. The difficulty is to get them to mix with the rest of the School freely and naturally – a difficulty increased by the fact that most of them live south of the river'. Shortage of money held back Paton's plans to raise standards. Although he found a school which had managed to sustain its high reputation in maths and classics, largely thanks to the teaching of the senior masters concerned, R. Tucker and G.F. Hawkes, UCS could not afford to buy the new equipment needed to give boys the quality of science teaching found at the best public schools. Paton tinkered with the school's creaking timetable, but barely touched the way in which the curriculum was organised.

A watercolour showing the site of the proposed school building in Frognal, 1905.

Although he was constantly on the lookout for premises for the school in Hampstead, Paton also found that UCS was still chained to University College. The affairs of the College were interfering with the effective management and development of the school. It was only in 1903 that a suitable site was identified, in Frognal, by which time Council, with pressure on the College resulting from proposals to reorganise the University of London, was at last forced to do something about it.

Paton, though, had had enough. He was succeeded by a friend of his. Harry Spenser, like Paton, came from Nottingham and had been a contemporary at St John's, Cambridge, where he had achieved a first-class degree. The fourth classicist in a row to head UCS, he too was only in his thirties when he was appointed. He came to UCS at the age of thirty-seven, from Glasgow High School, where he had been rector for four years. There was no doubting that Council had made a good decision. One of the High School's governors wrote that as rector Spenser had believed in his boys and interested himself in all their activities. He was a keen sportsman, enjoying rowing, cricket and fives. He had restructured the Glasgow school, modernised the curriculum and expanded extra-curricular activities. To Council, with approval given for the relocation of the school, Spenser's achievements made him the man of the moment.

Harry Spenser, headmaster 1903–16.

Spenser was very different from Paton. Neat, formal, dignified, almost a dandy in his dress, with a clear voice and piercing glance, he rarely relaxed his bearing. With a great grasp of detail, he took firm decisions rapidly and, it was said, 'was rather prone to ride roughshod over opposition – in short, his personality was of the most uncompromising kind'. This often gave rise to clashes with Council, especially later in his headship, as a decisive head grew increasingly irritable with a governing body more inclined to defer and delay.

He was not a good teacher of small boys, but was capable of inspiring senior boys. His lessons, wrote de Sola Pinto, were 'exciting, stormy affairs'. Spenser breathed life into masterpieces of classical literature through the depth of his knowledge, quoting at will from English literature to illustrate parallels between the ancient and the modern. His lessons, said de Sola Pinto, 'opened up new worlds of intellect and the imagination for the schoolboys who had the good fortune to hear him'. Spenser encouraged a generous intellectual open-mindedness and a respect for the opinions of others.

His apparent remoteness and his tendency to brief fits of violent anger obscured the fact that he was at heart a kind man with a strong sense of justice. A strict disciplinarian, he detested corporal punishment. The experience of one boy illustrates Spenser's humanity and sympathy for what UCS stood for. K.R.A. Hart, the son of a Russian Jew, was diagnosed at an early age as suffering from cerebral spastic diplegia, which severely affected his balance and his ability to walk. In an era when many disabled children were written off,

Spenser warmly welcomed Hart into the school, took a personal interest in his progress and, with the boys, accepted him for who he was, almost entirely overlooking his disability. Hart eventually won an exhibition to Oxford.

Spenser arrived at UCS determined to push through the improvements Paton had only contemplated. Paton had warned him that the curriculum within the school was in chaos and so Spenser found out, discovering that sometimes masters could be teaching a class for a whole term on the wrong scheme of work. The tradition of boys deciding for themselves which subjects to take was abandoned. Carrying on in this way, Spenser told Council, was 'to admit that every parent has an indefensible right to have his boy badly educated', and would only 'perpetuate existing inequality of attainment in the various subjects'.

Spenser's aim was to secure an all-round education for every boy. He described as 'folly' the practice of restricting a boy from the outset to those subjects in which he displayed any talent. The headmaster's hand was strengthened by the reforms being made in English education, particularly the recently introduced Regulations for Secondary Schools. He was able to introduce to UCS the system already in widespread use in many other secondary schools, where boys followed a common course for their first three years and then pursued one of several varied courses, designed to cover the needs of all boys in the school. The senior curriculum was divided initially into Commercial, Modern, Science and Classical sides; but the Commercial side was soon discontinued and the Modern side combined with the Science side.

Spenser appeared to have introduced to UCS the foundations of a modern education programme. There was one particular weakness. In contrast to what had gone before, each boy remained in the same form and there was no division into sets at all. The school had gone from one extreme to another. While the system adopted by Spenser was prevalent in Germany and used in many English elementary schools, there were doubts about its efficacy at UCS. It depended on consistent standards. This was difficult to achieve at UCS, where there was little steady pattern of learning among boys admitted from a wide range of different schools and at different ages.

One way in which Spenser tried to overcome this problem was to bring the school into line with the Board of Education's Regulations. This would allow it to apply for recognition from the Board, which was essential for the school to become eligible for financial aid from the Board. As it turned out, the school declined to pursue this. The Board wanted UCS to reduce its fees and this the school felt unable to accept. Throughout its history the school, liberal and independent, never felt much at ease in financial partnership with the state.

Spenser used recognition as a spur to improvement though. One requirement was to find more time for science teaching. This led to the resumption

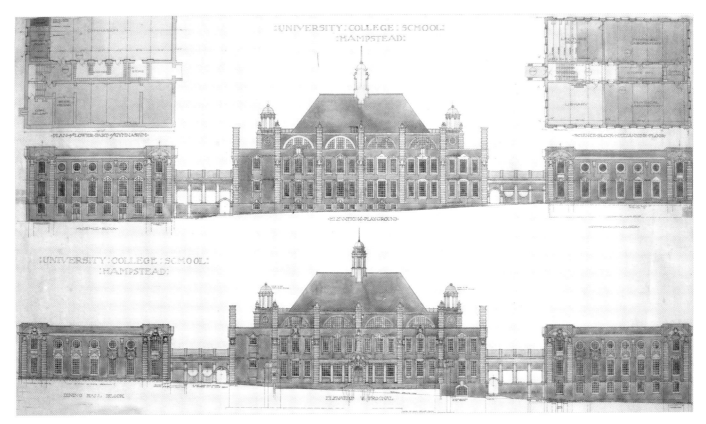

Plans for the new School were drawn up by Arnold Mitchell, 1905.

of Saturday-morning school. Jewish boys, absent through observance of the Sabbath, received an average mark. This was not popular with a number of Jewish parents and at least one boy was removed from the school before the change was reversed in 1911. As another facet of Spenser's aim to raise standards – trying to take in LCC scholars who would benefit from an academic education – the Commercial side, with which the school had never felt comfortable, was also abolished.

Spenser attacked other aspects of school administration. He updated, revised and consolidated the messy mishmash of school rules, many of which he found trivial and outmoded. He abolished monthly reports, regarding them as an excessive burden on staff. He also attempted to streamline school management so that the head was no longer bothered with a plethora of queries about minor issues. Here he was less successful – lack of cash and thus lack of support staff meant that the head continued to be a general factotum.

In the summer of 1904 the school was told that a site in Frognal had been chosen for the new school buildings. A design competition was won by the gifted Arts and Crafts architect Arnold Mitchell. The school would rank among his best work, alongside the department of agriculture in Cambridge. A central block was based around an imposing great hall, with a capacity for 1100, with twenty-four classrooms opening off the hall and off the first-floor

Front view of the School from *The Gower*.

University College School and the University of London were officially separated by the Transfer Act of 1905. Shown here is the seal of the College Transfer Commissioners designed by Eric Gill.

Sir Edward Durning-Lawrence contributed to the building costs of the new School and the great hall bears his name.

gallery. There were two wings – the north would house juniors, the south seniors. The north wing would also include a gym, with baths and changing rooms, plus a dining hall on the first floor. In the south wing there would be science classrooms and laboratories, a library and provision for the school monitors and the cadet corps.

Physical separation from University College symbolised the severing of ties between UCS and UCL. In 1905 the University College London (Transfer) Act, embodying this change, received royal assent. A new independent governing body, albeit with the same name, was created, including eight members from the previous Council, plus additional representatives from the universities, local authorities and other bodies.

The big question was how the school could afford to move. Costs were estimated at around £100,000 (£7.2 million today) and the school had to find half this money from fund-raising. Economies were made in the use of materials, while the panelling in the great hall was paid for by Sir Edward Durning-Lawrence, a former pupil, prosperous industrialist and politician, after whom the hall took its name. The site proved to be fiendishly difficult to build on. It was riddled with underground springs, and to forestall flooding of the main floors a substantial crypt had to be created. This extra expense, coupled with the cost of stronger foundations needed to cope with shifting subsoil, amounted to an additional £20,000 (almost £1.5 million today). The Council of University College contributed £60,000 towards the scheme. Unfortunately, the school secured only £8000 from fund-raising. The remaining debt of £52,000 (£3.7 million in current values) left the school financially crippled for years to come.

The first sod was cut on 15 May 1905 and the foundation stone was laid on 25 July 1906. The buildings were completed in time for an opening in the summer of 1907. Light and spacious, compact and efficient, the new building drew praise for gathering together almost every part of the school under one roof, unlike many others. The hall quickly became an important part of the school, not just because it was an impressive space for school events, but because it proved to be a focal point for boys and staff to meet as they passed from one side to another. Mitchell's main regret was that funds did not stretch to provide the garden setting he wanted at the rear of the school.

UCS said goodbye to Gower Street on 25 July 1907. The opening of Frognal took place the following day. It was a grand and royal occasion. The school was opened by the king, Edward VII, accompanied by his consort, Queen Alexandra, and their daughter, Princess Victoria. Crowds lined the streets outside the school to catch a glimpse of the royal party. The king reviewed the corps, drawn up smartly outside, and after opening the main door with a golden key, entered the great hall to the sounds of the national

anthem. The king gave a brief speech about the importance of education and, to popular acclaim, requested an extra week's holiday during the summer. After tea in the refectory, the royal party finally departed by the gate the king later agreed to be called the King's Gate. He also permitted the school to continue to display in the great hall the royal coat of arms made for the occasion and to place his statue in the niche over the front door.

The grand opening of the school, July 1907. All Hampstead came to view the ceremony performed by King Edward VII.

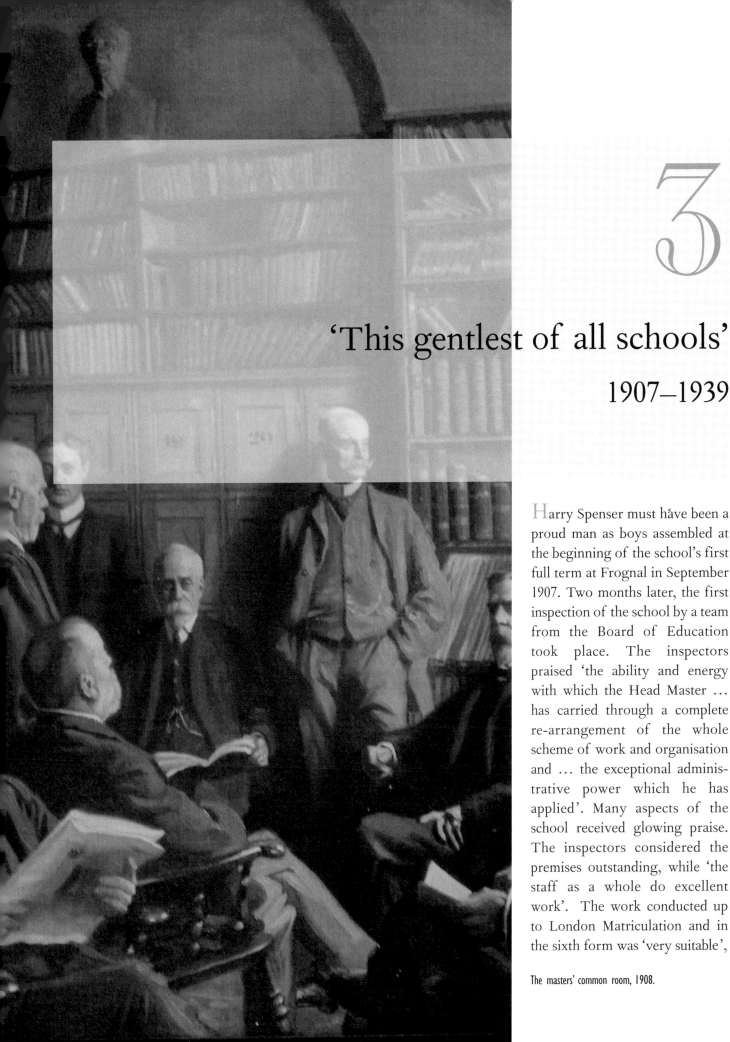

3

'This gentlest of all schools'
1907–1939

Harry Spenser must have been a proud man as boys assembled at the beginning of the school's first full term at Frognal in September 1907. Two months later, the first inspection of the school by a team from the Board of Education took place. The inspectors praised 'the ability and energy with which the Head Master … has carried through a complete re-arrangement of the whole scheme of work and organisation and … the exceptional administrative power which he has applied'. Many aspects of the school received glowing praise. The inspectors considered the premises outstanding, while 'the staff as a whole do excellent work'. The work conducted up to London Matriculation and in the sixth form was 'very suitable',

The masters' common room, 1908.

The refectory in the new school, 1907, 'a thing of beauty and joy from the first', according to *The Gower*, 1907.

and a basis for further growth. Noting the absence of corporal punishment, the inspectors reported that 'discipline seems to be maintained without trouble and punishments are rare'. 'While great freedom is left to the boys', they continued, 'they are trained in the habits of self-discipline and responsibility'. They singled out the level of pastoral care. This was now carried out through the house system which Spenser had overhauled. Still with Greek or Arabic letters for names, the school was now divided into six houses, later increased under Spenser's successor to eight. It was in a way a reversion to Eve's Consults, except that Spenser's houses conformed to the usual system, with the houses being responsible for sporting and pastoral care. The inspectors remarked on the positions of real responsibility occupied by the house masters, who acted as 'special counsellors' to each of the boys throughout their school life and dealt directly with parents. Corporate life, based on the houses, games and societies, was 'most vigorous' and of 'unusual excellence', while an 'excellent tone' was 'apparent in all parts of the school'.

46

With hindsight, there were warning signs in the report. Spenser, obviously overworked, had been granted leave of absence for a term. The huge debt shouldered by the school prevented any improvement in the poor salaries paid to staff. Without endowments, the school was reliant entirely on fees, yet much of this income was absorbed by servicing debt. Most boys, a large number of whom were making long journeys to Hampstead from all over London, were still leaving at fifteen or sixteen to enter business. The inspectors agreed with Spenser that many of the LCC scholars were unsuitable for an academic education at UCS. In contrast, there were only four boys in the classical sixth form and the number of those proceeding to university was 'smaller than is usual with a school of this standing'. In order to appeal to parents in North London, the inspectors felt that the school needed a 'classical tradition', which ran rather counter to everything the school had stood for.

Seven years later, the problems hinted at in 1907 were brought into the open by a further inspection. Spenser appeared to have retired into his shell, since the inspectors concluded that the head should do more to delegate routine tasks and use his time 'in actually visiting his colleagues at work and in giving them the criticism, guidance and stimulus they inevitably need'. The inspectors privately sympathised with Spenser, who was entirely responsible for and, in their view, overwhelmed by managing the school's financial problems. The school could not afford an assistant for him, so Spenser's ability to delegate was severely restricted.

Financial problems meant that UCS remained largely reliant on its bankers, although the latter expected no repayment of capital until numbers increased. In fact, Sir Edward Durning-Lawrence repaid £8000 (the equivalent of more than half a million pounds today) out of his own pocket. He had promised to do more, but this route to financial salvation disappeared with his sudden death in 1914. By the end of the year, after the second inspection, things were so bad that the head and his staff voluntarily gave up 20 per cent of their salaries, in excess of £160 a year.

The school desperately needed more boys. Without more boys, there could be no more income. It had been built to hold 720, but in 1914 it had fewer pupils than in 1907, just 352 boys. This was not helped by dithering on the part of Council over what to do about LCC scholarship boys. Spenser wanted to keep them but reduce their numbers and accept only the more able boys, who would not only benefit from an education at UCS, but would also raise the school's standards. Council concurred, but failed to reach any agreement on this way forward with the LCC. As a result, the school stopped taking any more LCC scholars, and the money that came with them, from November 1910.

There was, however, another element behind this decision. One reason Spenser wanted to change the admission of LCC scholars was that he believed

Front cover of prospectus.

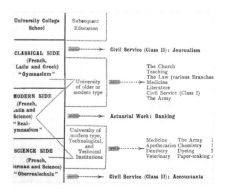

Detail from the prospectus showing various careers open to a boy.

that their poor quality lowered the tone of a school supposed to be providing a liberal education equal to the best public schools. He believed that many of those who might send their sons to the school were prejudiced against it. They did not want their well-bred sons to mix with so many boys from poor backgrounds. Spenser found this snobbery extended even to some Old Gowers, commenting bitterly that these were the people who were 'supposed to have early learned the invaluable lessons of tolerance and charity'. Yet he felt they could not be offended because they were such a likely future source of both boys and benefactions. These attitudes were not unusual for the time. The *Manchester Guardian*, having run an editorial in March 1911 criticising UCS's decision to stop taking LCC scholars, received several indignant replies. One headmaster wrote that 'the real difficulty is not the social or pecuniary inferiority of the elementary boy but his enormous moral inferiority'; another letter writer, signing himself 'Public School Boy', declared that it was 'more probably that the sons of gentlemen will be levelled down rather than the sons of Pork Butchers levelled up by continual daily contact. The lessons of the gutter are more easily learnt than the traditions of caste'.

Prejudice against the school was not confined to snobbery, however; it also extended to racism. There was a feeling locally that the school had too many Jews. Spenser reported to Council that 'the reproach against the school in the past has been that it has been largely composed of Jews and LCC

Harry Spenser with pupils, 1915.

House M, summer term 1915. The three teachers are Captain Scott-Lowe, Mr Cockman (centre) and Mr Paddock.

Scholars'. This was a line peddled by many Hampstead prep schools, still resentful about Holly Hill, and now sending fewer boys to UCS. But Spenser believed strongly that Holly Hill should be developed to counteract this attitude and fulfil its role to supply UCS with boys. Council seriously considered its closure to save money. Spenser's opposition was one reason this never happened, combined with the support of the inspectors in 1914, who pointed out that the Junior Branch was doing very good work and sending to UCS some of its very best boys.

From the experience of Holly Hill boy Kevin Fitzgerald, who left the school in July 1915, it was a happy place where boys were brought up in a tolerant atmosphere and encouraged to learn for themselves. Charles Simmons, recalled Fitzgerald, was convinced that all his boys were 'filled with moral earnestness, a desire to better the whole world, to lead a good life, to matter'. Under the influence of Simmons, of Miss Fuller, of Miss Aird, and other Holly Hill staff, young Kevin 'felt at home'. At Holly Hill, as at Frognal, 'the opinions of all men and women were considered to be of value; their religious beliefs were of the first importance but their own personal affair and always worthy of respect; a serious mind was everything and a flippant approach to life nothing'.

Some of the Old Gowers who were killed in the First World War. FROM TOP: Lieutenant-General Eric Miall-Smith; Lieutenant Marcus Segal; Second Lieutenant A.L. Wells.

LCC scholars represented 20 per cent of the school roll. As they dwindled, Spenser did succeed in replacing them with other boys. By 1914, in spite of any local opposition or bad feeling, more than 80 per cent of boys were from Hampstead or nearby, compared with a proportion of two-thirds when the school opened. In the face of other factors, including competition from other schools, this was quite an achievement. The difficulty was that UCS needed at least 600 boys and had little more than half that number.

Spenser must have felt under siege, since he was also failing to achieve the rise in standards he so desired. The school's financial woes were one reason. In 1914 the inspectors expressed 'grave anxiety' about the school's financial stability. The inspectors found that UCS 'cannot, for lack of money, attain the high pitch of efficiency at which it ought to aim'. UCS still had to take in boys at all ages, regardless of academic attainment.

With poor pay producing an 'absence of men of outstanding ability on the staff', the teaching was mixed, to say the least. The report on music, for instance, concluded that 'it is difficult to understand why the singing should be made as unpleasant to listen to as possible'. Staff were overstretched and Spenser himself was teaching as many as thirty-two hours a week. Vivian de Sola Pinto considered teaching at UCS was in a period of transition. There were the older men, who 'were obviously tired and cynical and held for the most part what I could describe as the penal view of education … whose main task was to keep the awful little creatures quiet and disciplined'. Perhaps it was men like this, dominating the teaching of the majority of boys who never reached the sixth form, who accounted for the degree of lethargy the inspectors found in the boys' approach to their work.

There were exceptions, such as Sammy Walker, whose literature classes were a delight; Freddie Felkin, the senior master and a fine classical scholar, whose lessons were full of excitement and interest; and younger staff such as mathematician Ulric Stanley and classicists Sydney Grose, soon leaving to take up university teaching at Cambridge, and Joey Meek, who had been placed ahead of the poet Rupert Brooke in the first-class honours list at Trinity College, Cambridge; Harry Spenser too seems to have found refuge in imparting his own classical learning, his love of language and relish for literature, to senior boys.

Lack of money also prevented Spenser from creating the leaving exhibitions he felt might have induced more boys to enter the sixth form. With seventeen sixth-formers in 1914, it was hardly surprising that the school should have had only eight Oxbridge scholarships over the previous two years. In the circumstances, all this seems something of a triumph against the odds. After all, whether by deliberate choice or bungled negotiations, the school was responsible for depriving itself of any LCC scholars at all.

For Spenser, the coming of the First World War was too much. Within two years there were just 300 boys in the school. The impact on the school of losses to staff and old boys can only have compounded his misery. Several staff joined up before Christmas 1914, but the first Old Gower casualties had preceded them: C.H. Rogers, only seven years after leaving UCS, died on 7 November from wounds received at Messines, while E.M. Ridge, of an older generation, was killed at Antwerp. The school lived up to its reputation for humanity and understanding when it took in almost thirty Belgian refugees, mainly from Brussels and Antwerp. The number of boys in the corps shot up, and even those who were not members took part in extra drills and parades. All away matches were cancelled for the duration and every house in school organised collections for Princess Mary's Fund to send Christmas presents to troops at the front.

Flippant comments from old boys at the front disguised acts of considerable bravery, many of them commemorated through awards for valour. The growing number of obituaries in *The Gower*, as the school magazine was called, lists promising athletes and musicians among the decent young men

C.H. Rogers, one of the first Old Gowers to die in the War.

The School took in refugees from Belgium, *The Gower*, December 1914.

Lieutenant E.C.M. Crosse was killed leading his men into attack in 1915. He was just 19 years old.

Officers' Training Corps contingent, 1912.

who had been killed. Lieutenant E.C.M. Crosse and Second Lieutenant Reginald Williams, killed leading their men into attack in May and September 1915 respectively, were just nineteen years old.

At UCS the Officers' Training Corps, or OTC as it was now known, was polishing up its shooting skills and won the Country Life miniature range shooting trophy in 1915. Boys spent part of their summers working on farms. The party sent to Rickmansworth in the summer of 1916 found that 'their knowledge of potatoes – in the field – and of stooking and threshing soon became extensive'. Speech day that year was marked, ironically, by a record number of four Oxbridge scholarships, but only endowed prizes were awarded, other winners receiving certificates to save money.

That was Harry Spenser's last speech day. At the age of fifty, he asked to resign in consideration of his health. He left, recommending his successor, and took up a post as an examiner for the Board of Education. In 1920 he was appointed headmaster of High Pavement School in his home town of Nottingham, where he remained until his retirement in 1928. He continued to keep in touch with boys he had taught at UCS until his death in 1937.

Guy Kendall was Spenser's nomination as his successor, and after interviewing two candidates, Council duly appointed him to take up the post of headmaster in the autumn of 1916. The fifth classicist in a row, he was also, at forty years old, the oldest man to be appointed headmaster. From a well-to-do landowning family, Kendall had been educated at Eton and Magdalen College, Oxford. Prizes marked every stage of his education, which culminated at

The OTC band plays the tank into action at Finchley Road, *The Gower*, 1916.

Oxford with firsts in classics and theology. He spent a year as warden of the Manchester University Settlement at Ancoats, taking up teaching after his marriage and arriving at Charterhouse in 1902. In the middle school at Charterhouse, Kendall liberalised the teaching of English. The poet Robert Graves later commented on the sympathetic understanding he received from Kendall as a pupil at the school. Denied the opportunity of promotion, Kendall began applying for headships, and on the third attempt came to UCS.

Perhaps more is known about Kendall's views on education than any other of UCS's early heads. Although school records for the time are sketchy, Kendall made his views known as a successful newspaper columnist, turning out dozens of articles for a wide range of newspapers and journals, from the *Daily Telegraph* and the *Daily Mail* to the *Evening Standard* and the *Sunday Express*. He also published his memoirs in 1933, three years before he retired.

Kendall, like his predecessors, favoured a balanced education, combining science with the humanities, and believed that the quality of teaching and the motive of learning were critical factors in inculcating intellectual habits. 'My idea', he wrote,

Guy Kendall, head from 1916 to 1936, known as 'Gussie'.

is of laboratories and schoolrooms stocked with appropriate objects likely to stimulate the curiosity and feed the imagination, with the scholars turned loose in them, and with masters in attendance holding a watching brief. The business of the schoolmaster is to awaken a purpose in his pupils, and to help them achieve it. That is the ideal.

But the teacher, Kendall felt, should strike a line between absolute laissez-faire and the excessively dictatorial. This happy equilibrium Kendall strove to bring to UCS, and one observer later recorded that it seemed that 'the boys of the UCS are dieted with liberty and authority in reasonably blended proportions'. This was very much in harmony with the way the school had been developed under previous headmasters.

Kendall was critical of the way boys were judged solely by their examination performance. 'We should not indeed be continually plucking up the plant to see how it is growing, but in a less formal and drastic way we should be continually examining without dissecting the plant at all.' Kendall was another head for whom each boy mattered. One newspaper profile of him in the 1930s suggested that he was 'far more interested in each separate boy … as an individual … He is interested in the individual boy with individual traits of disposition, requiring sympathy and consideration, and individual ability or talent (present, generally, although often latent), requiring development or nurturing'.

In much of his educational philosophy, Kendall, who became known as 'Gussie', seemed made for UCS. His liberal concept of religion was also in tune with the ethos of the school. Religion, he wrote, should be seen as 'the meeting point of all the values; to realise God as the source of beauty and truth (including the truth of science) as well as moral goodness'. Prayers had featured in morning assemblies under Spenser; this continued under Kendall, but, as one former pupil later remembered, his assemblies were always based on the Old Testament out of consideration for the large number of Jewish boys in the school.

Kendall's greatest immediate challenge was to overcome the problem which had defeated Spenser. The school was impoverished, heavily in debt, lacking endowments, without state aid and entirely reliant on fees. More boys were needed simply to bring in the income required to repay debt, let alone covering the improvements necessary for the school's progress.

Little could be done while the war continued. As casualties mounted, the headmaster carefully cut out and pasted every obituary of an Old Gower that appeared in the press. The toll was heartbreaking. Among the dead was Lieutenant John Hamer, killed in action on 22 March 1918 at the age of twenty, a former school captain, member of the 1st XV and 2nd XI, and winner of a Cambridge science scholarship. On 4 November 1918, in the last days of the conflict, Lieutenant 'Dicky' Grant died after his plane was shot down; he had left UCS in April 1917, a house captain, monitor, ace rugger player and dashing batsman. The school's VC winner, Sergeant Martineau, living in New Zealand at the outbreak of war, returned to the forces, gained a commission, served in Europe and returned to die in Dunedin in April 1916 after contracting fever in Gallipoli. By the time peace returned, 1556 Old Gowers had served in the war, 250 former pupils and 7 staff had lost their lives and 309 had been wounded. Two of the dead had been captains of monitors, still at school when war was declared. Eight captains and fifty members of the 1st and 2nd XVs between 1906 and 1916 had died. There had been 315 awards for gallantry, including 111 Military Crosses. A War Memorial Fund was opened and on 3 March 1922 the memorial, designed by Sir Edwin Lutyens, who also designed the Cenotaph, was unveiled by Major General Sir Theodore Fraser. The balance of the funds was set aside to help finance the education of sons of those Old Gowers who had died.

At the end of 1918 there were 319 boys at UCS and 137 at the Junior Branch, scarcely more than in 1915. Within a year this had grown to 397 and 210 respectively, beginning a steady rise in numbers that eventually settled at just over 500 for UCS and around 200 for the Junior Branch.

At the Junior Branch Charles Simmons was replaced as head by Bernard Lake, another member of staff from UCS, in 1919. Simmons, known to his staff as 'Simmy', had instilled in the school a happy, tranquil and good-humoured

John Hamer was killed in the final year of the war. While at UCS he had been school captain, member of the 1st XV and winner of a Cambridge science scholarship.

The War Memorial, designed by Sir Edwin Lutyens, was installed in the great hall. It was destroyed in the terrible fire of 1978.

Games committee with Bernard Lake (Bunny), the Head of the Junior School, sitting middle front row.

atmosphere, through the gentleness of his own character and his deep interest in everyone around him. Dr Lake, known as 'Bunny', held the reins until 1945, maintaining the ethos begun by Simmons. One of his quirks was his 'hasta sacra', an assegai that accompanied him into assemblies and became a school tradition. He was ably supported by loyal and long-serving members of staff like Miss Hooper, who taught crafts and mathematics for twenty-seven years until 1937, and Miss Fuller, who retired in 1939 after thirty-eight years of service, as well as by those he appointed himself, including Harry Byrom, C.E.F. Smaggasgale and Richard Trendell.

The sudden influx of boys into the Junior Branch after the war caused a few problems. Indiscriminate admission, for instance, necessitated the introduction of entrance tests in the early 1920s. More importantly, the ancient buildings, dating from the seventeenth century, were feeling the strain of accommodating too many young boys. Boys were instructed to wear plimsolls for fear the building should collapse around them. Senior boys were transferred to Frognal because of lack of space. Despite UCS's financial problems, Council no longer needed convincing of the value of the Junior Branch to the school as a whole. Bravely they determined – with rather more decisiveness than they had displayed previously – to buy the existing property. Two years after this was completed, in 1925, they decided, even more courageously, to press ahead with the construction of entirely new premises. The old building was demolished (it seems unlikely this would have

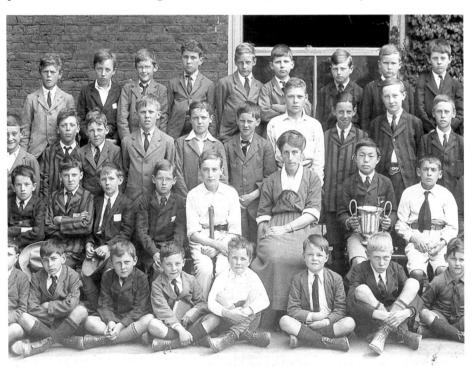

Junior Branch, 1920s.

been allowed today), but not before the panelling, staircase and front door had been salvaged for incorporation within the new premises. Designed by Sir John Simpson, the building was officially opened in November 1928, allowing the return of those boys who in the interim had been crammed into Frognal, most of them taking their lessons in the gym.

The finance for the new buildings came from a £20,000 loan (£800,000 today). This was added to the balance of £48,000 outstanding from building the Frognal premises. In addition, loans had been taken out to buy and improve the new playing fields, as well as the original Holly Hill building. The annual interest charge by 1927 was £6000 a year (£240,000 today). Brave though Council had been, the burden of debt was a major hindrance to the development of UCS. Any additional income was welcome, and for this reason the decision had been taken immediately after the war to make an application for funding from the Board of Education. The application was successful and the extra £3000 a year proved invaluable. A year later, Council also applied for a deficiency grant from the London County Council.

This application was also granted and once again scholarship boys, this time from Middlesex County Council as well as London County Council, were admitted to UCS. One of the reasons for the application had been the attraction of boosting pupil numbers. By September 1921, scholarship boys formed almost a quarter of the school's annual intake. An analysis of the intake for that term shows that twenty-two out of a hundred boys were scholarship boys. They came mainly from Hampstead (twenty-eight) and the county of Middlesex (forty-three), with the next largest group (nineteen) coming from Islington, Marylebone and St Pancras. A quarter came from working- and lower middle-class backgrounds. Their fathers included railway workers, printing workers, market porters, clerks, joiners and postmen. There were thirty-one boys whose fathers worked in business and commerce, twenty-seven from a professional background and a handful whose fathers were in the arts, media and teaching. Half a dozen had lost their fathers in the war. As the headmaster stated to Council in his report for 1924–25:

we have, I think, a very sound assortment of typical English boys in the School; they may justly be said to represent every 'social stratum' and thus be the epitome of English society… they are a delightful set of boys and, in their general quality, one of which any School might justly be proud.

This breadth of background remained the case until the scholarship boys disappeared from the school in the late 1960s.

This mixture, combined with 'the gentle spirit of the head master and most of the staff', explained for Stephen Spender, a pupil from 1923 to 1927,

Junior Branch, 1920s.

The new Junior School opened in 1928, designed by Sir John Simpson.

Stephen Spender attended the School from 1923–27. He described it as 'this gentlest of all schools'.

Mr Druce, senior English master.

what he described as 'this gentlest of all schools'. Spender, whose education had been unhappy before he reached UCS, argued that 'the sons of the wealthy and the finely bred in England are often dominated by a certain harsh exclusiveness', a competitiveness in everything, a hostility towards individuality. Working-class boys, on the other hand, lacked such jealousy and, he found, respected excellence in individuals, an abiding characteristic of the school. They also taught him 'to understand the lives of those who were poorer than myself'. By the time Spender left UCS, he appreciated how his opinions were respected, whereas at Oxford he found students from public schools sneering at his aestheticism and indignant at his socialism. 'I felt far freer at UCS than I ever did in the snobbish environment of Oxford'.

At first, not many of these additional boys could be persuaded to stay at school beyond the age of sixteen. There were fewer than 50 in 1920 (there had been 112 in 1914) and, with 119 in 1928, they still represented a smaller proportion of boys than before the war. Even to achieve this, Kendall had had to continue admitting boys up to the age of sixteen, and by the late 1920s was doing so regardless of whether they had attained standards expected of their age group. He regretted that UCS still did not appeal to the more prosperous residents of Hampstead and felt, like Spenser, that they were deterred by the presence of county scholars and, even more so, as he reported to Council, by 'the religious and racial circumstances of some boys'. Whether or not he knew it, there was some snobbery about scholarship boys among older members of staff. One pupil recollected how Mr Druce, the senior English master, with a tyrannical reputation, 'had, it seemed, his knife into the council scholars'. Once, instructing boys that 'height' was correct and 'heighth' was wrong, he shouted, 'Common and ignorant people say "heighth"; Livermore [a scholarship boy] says "heighth"'.

Kendall, however, saw no reason to apologise for any boy in the school. Although he eventually changed his mind, he believed initially that county scholars would hold their own socially and intellectually. He was also happy to admit Jewish boys and responded furiously to an unjustified accusation of anti-Semitism made in a Jewish journal in 1922. The journal alleged that UCS had preferred a boy of British-born parentage to one whose father had been born overseas. Kendall quickly and firmly denied that this had ever happened. It would certainly have gone against the grain of past practice at the school, which was perpetuated in the 1930s when the school admitted a number of German Jewish refugees fleeing from Nazism. One of those boys, Ernst Sondheimer, later recalled that 'the school was a release and a revelation; in its liberal atmosphere there was no trace of prejudice against me as a German and a Jew'.

Kendall battled hard to persuade parents to allow their boys to stay on in the sixth form, but to little avail. Sixth-form membership grew only slowly,

and fencing were available, rowing and fives were revived. The fives team won the first Schools of England Rugby Fives Challenge Cup in 1923, although only four teams competed because of short notice. The boat club, formed in 1926, flourished despite often straitened finances, chalking up successes in fours against Westminster and Eton. In 1931 the club took over premises on the river at Richmond, with its own boatman, and four years later acquired its first two (albeit second-hand) eights. The school centenary appeal, hindered by the desperate economic depression, raised funds towards a swimming pool. Progress was slow, but the pool was finally completed during 1936.

Kendall, with his own experience of the Ancoats settlement, maintained links between the school and what became known in the 1920s as the Bermondsey Boys' Club. This lasted until 1930, when the school transferred its allegiance to another settlement on the Isle of Dogs, known as the Docklands No. 2 Settlement, founded in 1923. Both clubs brought a taste of a different world into the lives of those UCS boys who became involved.

A sense of responsibility towards others was fostered in other ways too. In 1928 the plight in the South Wales coalfields led the boys to collect clothing

Mr Wallis (centre) with the rowing team.

A UCS eight on the Thames at Richmond. The boat club had premises here from 1931 and employed a boatman.

The School Centenary Appeal raised funds for the School's first pool, which opened in 1936.

and other articles for families in straitened circumstances. In the following year weekly form collections raised funds for a secondary school in another distressed area. The money was used to buy school dinners for those in need at the James I Grammar School in Bishop Auckland in County Durham. In the mid-1930s UCS also took part in a scheme which allowed boys in the local area to use the West Hampstead playing fields during school holidays.

Towards parents Kendall had an ambiguous attitude. He held occasional meetings with them throughout his headship, but he never had any hesitation in reprimanding them if he thought their actions were detrimental to the education of their sons. He felt deeply the duty of care the school owed towards the boys and the responsibility of preparing them through their education for the rest of their lives. In this regard, UCS was enlightened for the times in having a policy on sex education. In March 1934 Council resolved that 'boys who have not been spoken to on the subject by their parents shall be spoken to by the Head Master or House Masters as may be arranged by the Head Master'.

Kendall was absent from school through illness during part of 1934, and at the end of 1935 announced his early retirement. He wrote in March 1936, towards the end of his last term, that 'the qualities of UCS that seem to me to stand out most are kindliness, tolerance, vitality, open-mindedness'. The consensus was that these qualities owed much to Kendall. Those who looked further back would have realised that Kendall was the latest custodian of values established during the early years of the school, but no head could simply sit back and expect that they would look after themselves. Kendall – and his predecessors – hoped to be like the first servant in the parable of the talents, taking what he was given and doubling it in value. The report in the local newspaper suggested that Kendall had succeeded, commenting that 'his breadth of outlook and sincere desire to try and see matters from the point of view of the boys have been a source of a pleasant atmosphere of freedom and tolerance at UCS'.

There was a view as Kendall retired, however, that the complacency affecting the classroom extended towards discipline throughout the school,

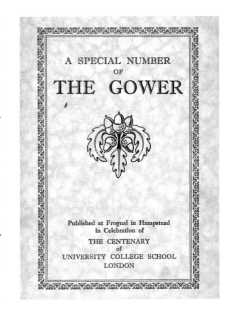

Centenary programme.

Old Gowers' rugby.

65

Guy Kendall at the opening of the craft block.

and that the balance between liberty and authority had swung too far towards the former. This seems to have been a view formed in retrospect and any firm evidence is wanting. There is, on the other hand, no doubt about the lack of direction which had crept into the teaching provided at UCS and the low expectations that staff had of boys. The inspectors noted that 'a good proportion of the boys are willing and intelligent and even the less able would probably respond better if more thought was given to the problem of how best to supply their needs'. There was little doubt that UCS needed revitalising and shaking out of its lethargy. This was something that Guy Kendall's successor certainly achieved.

The next classicist in his thirties to head the school was Cecil Simpson Walton. He was thirty-one when he was appointed and among the youngest heads of his generation, alongside Jack Wolfenden, aged twenty-seven when he took over as head at Uppingham in 1934, and Robert Birley, appointed to Charterhouse in 1935, aged thirty-two. The son of a vicar, he was educated at Rugby and Balliol College, Oxford, where he achieved a first in classics. After studying abroad at the British School in Rome and the University of Vienna, he returned to England to teach briefly at his old school before moving to Westminster School as master of the seventh form and senior classical master in 1930.

Walton, known as 'Fruity' after a well-known chain of greengrocers and fruiterers with the same name, came to UCS with the certainty and confidence of a young man in his prime. Full of energy and vitality, he set off at a breathtaking pace to stamp his own impression on the school and his enthusiasm encouraged others. He was seen so often around the school by the boys, many of whom had rarely set eyes on Kendall, that he was popularly believed to have several doubles. Often kind, affable and charming, his priority was the interests of each boy (one of his first feats was to learn the name of every one of them), and anyone or anything that stood in the way of what he believed should be done was cast out of his consciousness. Walton knew what he wanted and settled for nothing less. The goals he set himself and the standards he aspired to made it hard for him to accept human failings in adults, with whom he could be ruthless, yet enabled him to turn a blind eye to them in boys.

He had an ambivalent attitude towards the school's past, professing a distaste for tradition, rewriting history when it suited him, or dispensing with it altogether, partly in an attempt to convince those new to the school – boys, parents or staff – that he was beginning with a clean sheet and that everything written on it came from his pen alone. He did this with remarkable success. Some boys, for instance, always believed that the venerable Task Book, which Walton retained, was his own creation. N.P. Cutliffe, school captain in Walton's first year, remembered how 'as if to underline his determination to make a clean break with the past, Walton ordered a clear out of relics of the Kendall regime. At the end of [the first] term, old papers and folders for disposal were piled in a corner of the hall'. But this attitude also created tensions, particularly with Old Gowers, one post-war secretary of the Old Gowers' Club later writing that at this time 'relations with the school were sometimes strained'. It did not help that he very soon abandoned use of 'Paulatim', the school song.

In fact, much of what Walton did, whether he was aware of it or not, harked back to what had gone before, reflecting strands of an ethos that stretched back more than a century, confirming that he was the right man in the right place. Indeed, while the motto of the period was said to be that 'the only tradition at UCS is to have no traditions', he himself acknowledged the value of tradition, once extolling, for instance, UCS's 'excellent tradition for freedom'. He had a talent for the unconventional, but used this as much to reinforce and reinvigorate convention as to create something new. His aim was always for excellence, not simply in academic affairs, although one of his

At work in the physics laboratory.

GREAT SCHOOLS IN SPORT

No. 50. UNIVERSITY COLLEGE SCHOOL

first decisions, confirmed by Council in the summer of 1936, was to raise admission standards, even at the expense of numbers.

If UCS had become too relaxed under Kendall, Walton was going to tighten things up. Some of his decisions were bound to upset both senior boys and senior staff. Walton seemed unconcerned. He insisted on emphasising recent shortcomings so that the bright new future would stand in even greater contrast to the immediate past. He made it known, in particular, that he believed that duties had been shirked in the name of tolerance. His comments on past events were often forthright, leaving no one in any doubt of what he really thought.

The surviving staff register from the 1930s shows the extent to which Walton believed he needed the support of new men in his campaign to raise standards. Between 18 January 1937, when a temporary handicraft teacher was recruited, to 21 September 1938, when David Black-Hawkins came to teach French and German, he made eighteen new appointments, representing nearly half of the total staff. Some of the surviving older staff were bewildered. 'Joey' Meek, for instance, as his obituarist recorded, 'found that he was expected to perform miracles and to perform them overnight, and his gentle, cautious temperament was no defence against the dynamic whirlwinds of CSW, who was seized with a sense of perpetual urgency, utterly foreign to Joey's character'.

Senior boys were also dismayed by some of the decisive steps taken by Walton while he was waiting for new boys to percolate through the school and come under his influence. He abolished the electoral college Kendall had created in 1921 to elect monitors. The influence of the college had spread over the years and it represented a barrier between the new head and the implementation of his aims.

On the other hand, the inspectors who visited the school in late 1937 were impressed by the speed at which Walton was turning things round and found that words could not describe how highly they rated the new head. And despite these changes, the atmosphere in the common room, remembered David Black-Hawkins, was free from the petty feuding that he had experienced at his previous school. His colleagues, although surnames alone always had to be used, were warm, welcoming, friendly and cooperative.

Detail of School, from *The Gower*.

FACING PAGE, CLOCKWISE FROM TOP LEFT: Gymnastics; basketball in the gym; the School as it appeared in *The Illustrated Sporting and Dramatic News* on 26 June 1936.

'Intelligent, sensitive, straightforward citizens'
1939–1955

For a man in a hurry, Walton must have found it frustrating to have a brake put on his plans by the Second World War. In an address to the old boys in 1947, the head was said to have described the war period as 'an enforced wait in which they could not do the things for which they had been preparing in 1938'. Walton tried hard to ignore it. He was determined that as little as possible should disrupt the school. Evacuation would have made it difficult for him to maintain his control, undone all the good work he had so far achieved and probably (as was the experience of a number of evacuated schools) produced a breakdown in discipline. He had already made this decision during the Munich crisis, insisting that

Final Call, *The Tempest*, 1946.

Towards the end of the war the bombing was particularly fierce with Hilter using flying bombs or VIs. 'These ghastly weapons came over at almost any time, flying low and noisily with their crude jet engines which, quite suddenly, cut out and the bomb quickly came down and exploded. Because of these missiles we sat our School Certificate papers in the shelter of the crypt. One morning, towards the end of exams, my home was hit. I managed to find some clothes in the wreckage but could not trace a school tie. Arriving at school in time for General Science III, feeling rather heroic, I was greeted by Fruity (the headmaster) with shocked, raised eyebrows, "No tie, Ettlinger?" '
Rev M. Brian Ettlinger, *The Gower*, 1995.

the school would remain in Hampstead unless otherwise ordered by the government. Early in 1939 the Board of Education approved Walton's plan for the school to stay in London on the grounds that it was on the fringe of so-called neutral areas, regarded as free from the threat of bombing. Walton believed that UCS was the only one of a thousand London schools to remain open.

There must have been anxiety among some staff and parents about the safety of the school once the bombing of London began in earnest. The boys took everything in their stride, waiting patiently in class for the signal from the master in charge to move to the crypt to continue their lessons when the siren wailed. 'To most of us,' remembered one, 'the war made little difference.' Most boys took the disruption, the uncertainty, the changed conditions, with equanimity. It was only when things began to return to normal that many of them recognised the hidden exhaustion caused by the war and realised they had been living on their nerves. The boys who suffered most were those sitting their exams during the years when air raids were at their peak, their evening studies disrupted by hours spent in the shelters, their exams disturbed by daytime raids.

With younger staff called up, long-serving staff, among whom were those Walton had upset most, faithfully kept the school going. Some even came out of retirement. Their experience of life gave them a sangfroid which kept spirits up. During the dark days of 1940, when Walton was tearing down from the noticeboard headlines about the downfall of France, one class of boys arrived in Ulric Stanley's class. Hearing that their previous teacher had been gloomily foretelling doom, he reminded them, before resuming his revision of Pythagoras, how he remembered Mons in 1914. Another member of staff gave many talks to crowded audiences, after Hitler's attack on Russia, about the USSR and its opposition to fascism. This was Dr John Lewis, who came to teach biology for the duration of the war. He was the sort of man UCS always seemed at home with: brilliant, passionate, learned and eccentric. An avowed Marxist, he had apparently been on the staff of the *Daily Worker*.

Walton did everything he could to take the boys' minds off the war. Away matches continued until it was impossible to find other schools to play against. One season, when the rugby team was left without a coach, Walton himself, with no previous experience, took on the role and coached them to success. Perhaps his most unconventional ruse, announced as a way of training the boys to ignore the distractions of war, was his deliberate attempt to disrupt

ABOVE: Cecil Simpson Walton, headmaster 1936–56.

Mr Vogel with the 2nd VIII rowing team, 1943.

the school exams sat by boys in the year prior to their official School Certificate examinations. This seems to have happened at least two years in a row. In the first year, masters climbed in and out of classroom windows, blowing whistles, letting off thunderflashes and stink bombs. In the following year, boys were told to remember a fictitious telephone number and code name, which was the only information they were allowed to reveal to any questioning member of staff. Between exams the boys had to swim the pool, run across the Heath and count the hens then kept by the school, trying to ignore a no doubt mystified 'Joey' Meek, who had been told to recite 'The Pobble who has no toes' as loudly as possible.

Occasionally it was impossible to keep the war at bay. In late 1940 several bombs fell either on or close by the school site and playing fields. Staff found their training in the extinguishing of incendiary bombs put to good use. There was little damage other than the bomb craters. Harold Flook, the chemistry master, on fire-watching duty one night, found himself surrounded by red-hot shrapnel after a bomb roared down on to the tennis courts. The crater created by the bomb was filled in single-handedly by the caretaker, Ted Shefford, respectfully known ever after by the boys as 'Hercules', a name apparently coined by Walton himself.

One boy, a captain of monitors a few years previously, returned to teach PE at the school after being invalided out of the navy with shell shock. He was

Makeshift classroom.

a reminder that other former pupils were losing their lives overseas. In 1941, for instance, John Reekes was lost at sea on his first voyage, at the age of sixteen. He and John Evans, who was killed in the RAF at the same time, aged twenty, had both left school in 1940. By 1945, of the 992 old boys on active service, 109 had been killed. Two boys who were still pupils at the school lost their lives in bombing raids. Eric Crowther, the friend of one of these, Tony Williams, recalled his distress at seeing his friend's ruined house from the bus to school one morning and then failing to find Tony at the bus stop as usual. The boy's body was later recovered from the chimney of the wrecked house.

During the summer months parties of senior boys attended harvest camps. In 1941 sixty-three boys and staff put in 4500 hours on seventeen farms over seventeen days. One boy recalled how the younger ones 'relied on the older boys to get us into pubs and order beer'. They hoed and weeded swedes – a monotonous task, apparently unrelieved, according to one boy, even 'by the most relentless of blonde land-girls' – and learned how to build and line up stooks of corn. The tradition of community service fostered by the Task Book was taken one step further during the war, when boys were required to

Boys worked on Harvest Camps during the War. Brian Ettlinger, a pupil at the time, remembered a camp at Holmer Green where he worked alongside very good-humoured Italian POWs. The following year they were replaced by 'rather sterner captives from Rommel's Afrika Korps.'

Bows and arrows on Hampstead Heath.

put in service at school in the absence of domestic staff, taking turns to wait on tables and clean the buildings, for example.

The position of the school was fundamentally changed in 1944. Under the Education Act pioneered by R.A. Butler, all fees for secondary education provided by the state were abolished. The only exception lay in the new category of direct grant schools, which, in return for state funding, continued to admit free of charge those boys recommended by local authorities. Corporation, a body created at the time of the separation from University College in 1905, essentially consisting of supporters of the school, mainly former pupils, but without any executive role, sent a letter of concern to the chairman of Council, then the Liberal politician and Old Gower, Sir Andrew McFadyean, arguing in favour of the school's continued independence. Council needed no convincing and passed an appropriate resolution at its meeting in November 1943 when the contents of the letter were raised. Council and Corporation were as one in believing that only independence would perpetuate what the letter described as the school's 'freedom of thought and discipline'. Council also agreed with Corporation that the Act and its consequences made it essential to place the finances of the school on a firmer footing. Corporation proposed that any memorial fund for the dead of the Second World War should have this as its primary purpose. Council responded that the school was seeking to raise £35,000 (the equivalent of a million pounds today) to that end. Although details are scant, the fund-raising seems to have been a success, judging from the fact that it was reported to have reached the halfway mark by the middle of 1944.

Given the school's continuing indebtedness, the appeal was absolutely essential. Freedom from the Board of Education also gave the school the ability to raise the level of fees, previously subject to agreement with the Board. In fact, taking inflation into account, fees in 1954 turned out to be little different from those charged in 1939. It was the appeal, together with the agreement of the trustees of remaining funds, which enabled the school finally to eradicate its debts in 1954, when the last £24,000 was paid off. What was not possible was to fund the major, and much-needed, improvements to the school's facilities in the immediate post-war years – as well as repaying the remaining debt, the retention of wartime controls over building made it impossible for UCS, as an independent school, to obtain consent for new works. Minor works were carried out, including the relaying of the

OTC, 1940s.

OTC foot inspection at Strensall.

TOP: Pupils working on the Memorial Garden.

BELOW: The dedication of the new war memorial combining the names of Old Gowers who died in the First and Second World Wars, 1980.

FACING PAGE: A crowd of over 80,000, including many UCS boys, converged on Hampstead Heath to watch a thrilling ski jumping competition in March 1950. A huge scaffolding was erected and snow was brought from Norway.

playground, the creation of new tennis courts, and the conversion of the crypt for locker use and of the former locker room to a second gym. A lot of this work was achieved through the use of working parties of boys, as Paton had once done, but paid at union rates, assisting the school maintenance staff. For instance, boys were used to bring to fruition Arnold Mitchell's vision of a garden setting for the school, work Walton had begun in 1937. The beautiful gardens, tended by Walton and his sister, who lived with him, provided a fitting backdrop for the memorial to those killed in the Second World War. Designed by Robert Lutyens, whose father had been responsible for the First World War memorial, the plaque recording their names was unveiled on 24 September 1949, when the memorial garden was dedicated. Some years later the names of those from both world wars were combined in the same memorial within the garden, dedicated by the Bishop of Rochester, himself an Old Gower, on 24 October 1980.

The stroke of genius in the aftermath of independence was Walton's negotiation with Middlesex County Council to continue admitting scholarship boys. This had three advantages for the school: it produced a guaranteed income, it helped to raise numbers (the roll had fallen to 300 during the war) and, with Walton having increased admission standards, it brought a stream of very able boys into the school. Walton would have all the advantages and none of the disadvantages of admitting scholarship boys that his predecessors would dearly have loved. The County Council was only too happy to participate; in the havoc created by the war and before the government's school-building programme got under way, there was a shortage of school places in London, making it relatively easy for UCS to build up its numbers fairly quickly once peace returned. By 1954 the total number of boys in UCS and the Junior Branch had reached 726, surpassing pre-war levels. Of these, 200 held free or assisted places from Middlesex County Council (the Council moved from free places to assisted places in 1952).

For Walton, the end of the war was almost like starting all over again. With the school only half full, he could fill it up with able boys coming within his sphere of influence for the first time (as Spenser had done), and create the strong sixth form he had always wanted. As headmaster, he must have felt even more secure and confident. He had been the unquestioned leader within the school throughout the war, almost autocratically so, in charge of a band of committed but largely elderly staff, many of whom would retire in the first years after the war. Most of the staff returning from the war were those he had recruited himself, while retirements enabled him to make more new appointments. By 1954 only seven of the school's twenty-nine staff had service prior to 1936, while eleven had been appointed since 1950; in other words, twenty-two had been recruited by Walton. A number of them were

ABOVE: Geoffrey Carrick, one of many masters who was educated at the School and returned to teach.

Front cover of *The Gower*, 1942.

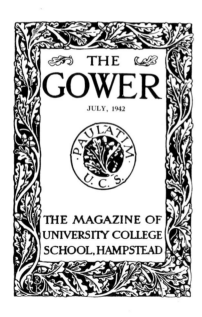

Old Gowers, who always had the feeling that they had been picked out by Walton early on in their school days for a return to UCS after university. Among these were Ivor Wilkinson and Geoffrey Carrick, who both returned from Oxford to teach at UCS, Wilkinson in 1946, Carrick in 1950.

Walton probably wished to appoint even more staff. A ratio of one member of staff to every fifteen boys was not regarded as generous, especially given the large sixth form. In 1954 every member of staff was apparently teaching every period of every day. But in the early 1950s the senior school, unlike the Junior Branch, was still recording an annual loss of more than a thousand pounds (£20,000 a year in today's values). Partly in order to save money, Walton acted as his own bursar, with the help of an accounts clerk. Shortage of money prevented the appointment of more staff and compelled Walton to make the most of the talents of existing staff, outside as well as inside the classroom. So the master who taught music at Holly Hill, Robert Strong, acted as caretaker at Frognal; Aubrey Morley was appointed to the classics staff on the understanding he would take over the orchestra; while Harold Flook assumed a long and varied list of duties.

While Walton possessed obvious charisma – evidenced by the vivid memories of him held by those who were at school during his tenure – he was a decidedly strange character. This is particularly clear in two sets of striking reminiscences of him, one written by a former pupil, Richard Pike, the other by Ivor Wilkinson. Walton kept his inherent instability in check only through the imposition of the utmost self-control. This characteristic was increasingly reflected in how he ran the school. He seems to have believed that the only way he could keep the school in order was by exercising the same extreme degree of control. For the boys this was not necessarily obvious; for staff, it became oppressively so.

One of the first times this manifested itself was in the way Walton decided to reorganise the house system within UCS. At the end of the war the influx of new boys provided the ideal opportunity to adapt the house system to changing circumstances once more. The previous system of eight houses had come close to collapse under the pressure of war, particularly with the virtual disappearance of house matches and the departure of many staff. Walton decided to strengthen the system by replacing the eight existing houses with four larger ones, enabling greater cohesion between boys of different ages. He refused to call them houses though; instead, in line with his aim of creating a classical ambience within UCS, they were called Demes, deme being the Greek word for parish. As the leading educationist Sir Will Spens pointed out at a later prize-giving, Deme was but another name for house. The word Deme was certainly more distinctive, however, indicating a break with the past and giving new boys a sense that UCS was different, as Walton probably intended.

Walton may have been thinking about the change for some time, but the first the heads of the existing houses knew about it was when all the house signs were taken down from classroom doors one break-time. The day became known colloquially as the 'Great Dissolution'. Two of the new Deme wardens, as house masters were now called, had been appointed by Walton, two had not. The former were David Black-Hawkins and George Baxter, who both joined the school in 1938. The other two were Harold Flook and Bertie Burrough, appointed by Kendall in 1933 and 1935 respectively. Each Deme took its name from its first Deme warden. Flook and Black-Hawkins spent the rest of their careers at UCS; Burrough and Baxter both left during Walton's term. Burrough left within a year of his appointment as a Deme warden, eventually running three schools and becoming president of the Headmasters' Association. When he went to the head's study to offer his resignation, Walton asked him to think about it; the two men sat in silence for an hour, neither one giving way. Walton regarded Burrough's departure, to be merely an assistant master elsewhere, as such a betrayal that Burrough was the only Deme to change its name (in favour of his successor, Mr Evans). Baxter left in 1953, but went on to a headship, which Walton regarded as acceptable. The wardens became the head's key lieutenants in the school, meeting with Walton three times each week over lunch, a system his successor continued.

George Baxter talking to a pupil in 1953.

Harold Flook epitomised the master Walton made the most of and felt he could rely on. He was head of chemistry, head of science, president of the boat club, Deme warden and, in succession to Dr Chanter, conductor of the annual choral society concert for twenty-five years. A warm and kindly man, he was a crisp and clear teacher, meticulous in his preparation, helpful to those who found the subject difficult and enthusiastic in the classroom. One colleague later observed that 'Harold always did demonstrations with the mildly embarrassed air of a schoolboy caught doing an illicit experiment after hours'.

Harold Flook, the epitome of the multi-tasking master; head of chemistry and science, deme warden, president of the boat club, conductor of the Choral Society and School organist. He was a pupil at the School from 1920 to 1927 and master from 1933 until his retirement in 1976.

The choral society concerts which Flook conducted from 1947, with a chorus made up of UCS boys, parents and staff, and later also girls from South Hampstead, became the only significant focus of musical activity in the school under Walton. The annual choral performance symbolised for Walton the coming together of the school as a community. In much of what he did he strove to create loyalty and a commitment to the school as a whole rather than to any individual member of staff, which he believed had been the case in the past from his partial reading of the school's history. Although he feared that any other repeated musical activity would fail to achieve the sustained excellence he always sought, this was a puzzling attitude from someone who, unknown to most, was a good pianist with a grand piano in his home. It also undid much of the good work done by Dr Chanter until his retirement in 1947.

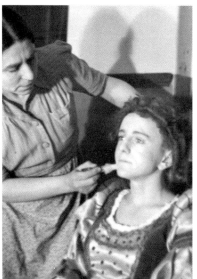

Walton had a similarly restrictive approach towards drama. There was a Shakespearian flourish after the Second World War, with striking performances of *Twelfth Night*, *Hamlet* and *The Tempest*, produced by the talented art master, Mr Wray. Brian Ettlinger gave a performance as Hamlet widely regarded as outstanding. Ettlinger was later a member of Donald Wolfit's company for a short period. Alongside Ettlinger was David McCallum, later to appear in the 1960s TV series *Man from Uncle*. But after 1947 there were no more school drama productions for nine years. The explanation was that Walton apparently could not bear to see boys playing parts, being other than themselves.

Walton shared with all his predecessors a belief in bringing out the full potential of each boy as an individual, although his methods in achieving this were rather different. His distaste for seeing boys achieve this as a mass or through any form of masquerade also led him to abolish what had become the Junior Training Corps in 1948, ostensibly on the grounds of falling interest.

One boy, whose school days overlapped the last days of the war and the first days of peace, believed boys weary from the turmoil of conflict turned more readily to sport than to clubs and societies. This might be one reason why societies were limited in their development during the decade after 1945. But it seems clear that over the years boys began to feel the lack of such activities. Ian McGregor, a first-class honours graduate in history from Cambridge, came from Manchester Grammar School to join UCS at the start of what turned out to be Walton's final term. He arrived aware of Walton's respected reputation as an educator and quickly warmed to the school's distinctive atmosphere. But he recalled, 'As a young master I became the focus for the evident wish of lively minded boys to get things going in the face of pervasive

Shakespearian drama flourished after the war:
ABOVE: D. Curry as Caliban in *The Tempest.*

FACING PAGE, CLOCKWISE FROM TOP LEFT: Ophelia in *Hamlet*; watching a play from the balcony in the great hall; Arthur, Robson and Duckett as elves in *The Tempest*, a backstage tour; boys in the back control box; Brian Ettlinger starred as Hamlet, 1946. Ettlinger went on to become a vicar; 'Shapes' from *The Tempest*, Mrs Butterfield making up her son Michael; B. Mayes as the ghost in *Hamlet.*

BELOW LEFT: Keeping amused backstage; RIGHT: Programme for *The Tempest.*

UNIVERSITY COLLEGE SCHOOL

THE TEMPEST

A Romance by
WILLIAM SHAKESPEARE

Saturday, December 13th, at 7
Mon., Tues., Wed., December 15th, 16th, 17th, at 7
1947

Price Sixpence

ABOVE: Roger Bannister, an Old Gower, broke the world record by running a mile in under four minutes in 1954.

apathy'. So he presided over the junior debating society, supervised the unofficial magazine compiled by the boys and began to make plans for the revival of drama. 'These were', McGregor recorded, 'all areas that were extremely dangerous to embark upon during Walton's later years. I might as safely have undertaken such liberal activities in Stalin's Russia.' Walton, in fact, was stung by criticism in the 1954 school inspection report, which lamented the absence of any drama in such a school and took note that McGregor had been involved in directing plays at Cambridge. It is safe to say that any plans Walton envisaged for drama were very modest.

Some sports introduced shortly before the war, such as hockey, failed to make a comeback, but others, long favoured at UCS, such as fives, did so successfully. The great Roger Bannister was at the school from 1944 to 1946, but, surprisingly for a school where the emphasis was on the development of individual talent, athletics was never really encouraged, and his running only seriously developed when he reached Oxford. A sailing club flourished briefly, with large parties taking to the water on the Norfolk Broads. During the 1950s the school eight under Hugh Cowham, ably supported by a first-class boatman, Harry Barnham, often beat the best schools in London. During the winter months, to give rugby a chance, membership of the boat club, which rose to 130 boys in the summer, was limited to 50 places. Under the coaching of Bryan Brown, appointed by Walton in 1948, the 1st XV, captained by John Barrett, achieved an unbeaten record the following season, generating renewed interest in the sport across the school. Barrett was a multi-talented sportsman, a good fly-half, an excellent left-handed batsman and, above all, a gifted tennis player. Brown, however, was one of those who never saw eye to eye with Walton and he left for another post in 1953.

John Phillips, appointed in 1949, took up the challenge with success. He was an impressive physical presence, who ran PE and the gym for many years. Under coach Jim Powell cricket was always popular, producing a couple of outstanding cricketers in John Slack, who later hit a century for Cambridge against Middlesex in 1954, and C.J. Parry, who captained Buckinghamshire in the Minor Counties Championship. The MCC team playing against the school in July 1950 included the famous Denis Compton, scoring a tentative nineteen runs while trying out his recuperating dodgy knee. Under coach Reggie Rands the school tennis team won the Glanville Cup in 1954. Boys were permitted to use the school tennis courts during the holidays, when they were also allowed to swim in the open-air pool and without supervision. The pool, completed before the war, was popular in the summer when the sun was out. A thermometer was dipped into the water to ensure the temperature had reached a minimum of 65 °F, although the boys were often sent in regardless. They swam in the nude, to the amusement of neighbours and the embarrass-

The swimming pool, 1951.

ment of visiting teams. For sensitive and self-conscious young boys, it must have been an ordeal, made worse after the war, when Walton had the walls surrounding the pool demolished, attracting groups of girls who assembled on the high wall at the back of school.

Walton had a sharp eye for talent when appointing staff and nowhere was this more evident than in the classics department, which became the academic bedrock of the school. Like several of his predecessors, Walton was a fine classicist. More than any of them, he exalted above everything else the language, literature, history and philosophy of Greece and Rome. They were the way that Walton intended UCS would achieve its academic reputation, the conduit through which boys from UCS would pour into Oxbridge and on to illustrious careers. The idea that there was no finer attainment for a young man than to achieve a classics scholarship to Oxbridge harked back to the nineteenth century and ignored the more recent trends that placed an equally high value on a much broader spectrum of subjects. But the number of classics scholarships achieved by a school was still regarded as an indication of its academic standing; moreover, in the eyes of many key employers, Oxford and Cambridge remained the only two universities which really counted.

At UCS Walton achieved his aspiration through the outstanding calibre of staff in the classics department. In 1946 Dr John Usher came to the school,

FACING PAGE, MIDDLE PICTURE: The tennis team, coached by Reggie Rands, won the Glanville Cup in 1954.

BOTTOM: A caricature of Reggie Rands on his retirement after 40 years at the School in 1959.

85

Aubrey Morley, shortly before his retirement, playing at the UCS Revue.

initially to work with the Junior Branch and the lower forms at Frognal, before taking up the full-time teaching of classics. An outstanding scholar, he was almost a caricature of a schoolmaster, with his flowing gown, his neatly combed and brilliantined hair, his immaculate appearance and precise, fastidious handwriting. He regarded those he taught as if they were a manifestation of his own personality, an expression of his own vanity. His teaching was dazzling, brilliant; one pupil who went on to All Souls never found anyone at Oxford who surpassed him. Five years later he was joined by Aubrey Morley, equally brilliant, modest, self-effacing, the kindest of men. By the time they retired in the early 1980s, after three decades of harmonious working, their pupils had achieved more than a hundred Oxbridge open awards. While Usher tended to confine himself to the classroom, Morley spread his talents throughout the school. He was a Deme warden, careers master, sixth-form tutor and conductor of the school orchestra. Both Usher and Morley, as men of great intellect, outshone their headmaster in the teaching of classics. Walton, it seems, was particularly jealous of Usher, who remained underpaid on a temporary contract until Walton had gone. Latterly the head, who continued to teach classics, would undermine Usher by talking about him in unprofessional terms to senior boys and encouraging them to subtly mock him.

Walton kept an eye on the progress of each boy as he made his way through the school, helped in this by his habit of rewriting reports for many boys. Apparently he was rarely satisfied with the way reports had been completed. This too produced an instance where he deliberately undermined a member of staff. John Hansford, the capable young maths master, refused

Members of the Junior Branch 1st XV rugby team, 1953.

to sign the reports rewritten for him by Walton. As a result, Richard Pike remembers that Walton instructed the boys taught by Hansford 'to play him up, ignore his instructions, not do his homework'.

The report system introduced by Walton in the early 1950s was an onerous one for staff. Every half-term each subject master wrote a detailed and confidential report on every boy, classified 'a' to 'e', which was discussed with each boy in the second half of term by his form master. The process was repeated at the end of term, with subject masters asked to confirm or modify their original comments. The end-of-term report was composed from these comments by the form master as a personal letter to parents. Nevertheless, this system was highly valued by staff and retained under Walton's successor. From this and his own observations, Walton was able to spot talented boys whom he felt had the potential to achieve places to read classics at Oxbridge.

There were instances, however, when he used his remarkable knowledge about every boy's abilities to divert them elsewhere in what he considered to be their best interests. Geoffrey Maitland-Smith and his brother Paul were at UCS during the late 1940s and early 1950s. Walton pointed Geoffrey, lined up for Oxford, towards accountancy, which he used as a springboard for a successful business career. Paul was discouraged by Walton from sitting his School Certificate on the grounds that failure would be soul-destroying for him. Instead, Paul's father helped him begin a lifelong interest and career in antiques.

Nevertheless, the entire organisation of the school, that is, both the Junior Branch and UCS, concentrated on fostering the talents of the most able boys through the study of classics. But the way in which Walton pursued his dream of academic excellence did have its drawbacks. The curriculum at the Junior Branch, emphasising classics at the expense of modern languages and science, was designed to mesh with the curriculum of the senior school.

Bunny Lake retired from the Junior Branch in 1945. He was replaced by C.E. 'Teddy' Vogel, Walton's closest colleague at UCS. Vogel had been appointed to UCS by Kendall in 1931 and became Walton's vice-master in 1940. But Vogel, while sharing Walton's aims, was a very different character, quiet, courteous, willing to listen and consult. He was surrounded by several existing dedicated staff, including Miss Hooper, C.E.F. Smaggasgale, Harry Byrom and Richard Trendell, who were joined by Vogel's own appointments, such as Jean Sladdin (later Mrs Smaggasgale), Barbara Hendrie, David Norman, Eric Marston, Michael Dean and John Marshall. For many boys, the person they could confide in at the Junior Branch was Reg Walker, the cockney caretaker. A former naval stoker, very short and very strong, with the ability to lift up several boys at once, he was a source of advice for anxious boys, as well as a scourge of bullies, a firm disciplinarian who never stood any nonsense. Under Vogel, sympathetic to Walton, but through his friendship

Top: 'Bunny' Lake retired from the Junior Branch in 1945.

Above: C.E. 'Teddy' Vogel.

Below: John Marshall, one of several dedicated and long-serving staff memebers at the Junior Branch.

Crafts room, 1950s.

left largely alone to run Holly Hill, the Junior Branch enjoyed a serene stability. Perhaps most importantly, Vogel's judicious selection of pupils for the Junior Branch played a crucial role in defining the nature of UCS itself as those pupils moved from one part of the school to another.

In pursuit of Walton's classical ambitions, the entry forms at UCS were divided between those who might have a talent for the classics, who studied Greek, and the rest, who studied history and geography instead. Those taking Greek were not taught any history and geography. A further weeding-out took place at the age of fourteen or fifteen. First came the brief informal interview with the headmaster. As Richard Pike remembered, 'Our talk with him was hardly a consultation, more a directive. I was still fourteen but from then on I knew I would study classics in the sixth form. It was as if Walton had picked his teams'. These boys found themselves sitting the School Certificate or its replacement, O levels, a year early; some boys were still fourteen. This in itself was not unusual for the time and, as far as UCS was concerned, enabled the school to compete with other public schools by giving boys three years in the sixth form. On the other hand, these boys found that their compressed course further narrowed the already limited horizons of their early education. Some of them received no teaching in either history or geography, nor in English literature, crafts or science. They were denied the opportunity of discovering for themselves whether they had an aptitude for anything other than a sixth-form arts course dominated by Latin and Greek.

The school inspectors noted in 1954 that some sixth-formers would not have received any teaching in history or geography since they entered the Junior Branch; it was hardly surprising, remarked the inspectors, that they 'sometimes show themselves strangely deficient in what might well be regarded as basic general knowledge of an historical or geographical nature'.

Other boys who had already passed their School Certificate or O levels prepared to enter the sixth form by spending a year (sometimes two, depending on the views of the head) in the UCS version of the lower sixth, known as transitus. They would have apparently coincidental encounters with Walton, who would quiz them on the subjects they intended to take for their Higher School Certificate. As they walked away, they would realise that, whatever their original intentions, the headmaster had made them change their minds – they were now taking classics, reading for a scholarship and headed for Oxbridge. One boy, who rejected Walton's advice and instead joined the family business, remembered how Walton told him he could have his pick of the Oxbridge colleges, regardless of the entrance exam. Another, John Slack, was surprised (as were his parents) to discover from Walton that he believed Slack should attend Cambridge. Walton was also happy to advise Slack's parents that their financial burden could be largely offset by grants from Middlesex County Council. For this, Slack reflected, he owed Walton 'a real debt of gratitude'. Slack was accepted into St John's College, in his own words, 'unseen and untested', simply on Walton's say-so. Thom Gunn, the poet, had a similar experience. He left UCS for Trinity College, Cambridge, and later reflected that 'Trinity was my headmaster's choice and to be honest it was amazing to me that I got in – it was solely on his recommendation'. This was still an age of patronage, when a well-connected headmaster could do much to ease the passage of his most able boys into the colleges of Oxford and Cambridge.

The academic vigour which pervaded UCS under Walton brought some outstanding results. University education in the 1950s remained the privilege of a tiny elite, but more and more boys from UCS were achieving membership of that select band. In 1953, for instance, when fifty-two out of ninety-eight sixth-form leavers took up university places, twenty-eight of them entered either Oxford or Cambridge, with the remainder joining London. Scholarships not only enhanced the reputation of the school, they also helped students to finance their studies when other sources of financial assistance were very limited. Apart from college and university scholarships, state scholarships had recently been introduced and were highly prized. In 1954 UCS boys won nineteen of these awards. In May 1955, when *The Economist*, in an early form of league table, listed those schools with the most Oxbridge scholarships and exhibitions, UCS, with eleven awards, lay in fifteenth position with Ampleforth, King's School, Canterbury and Shrewsbury.

Deep concentration in the crafts room.

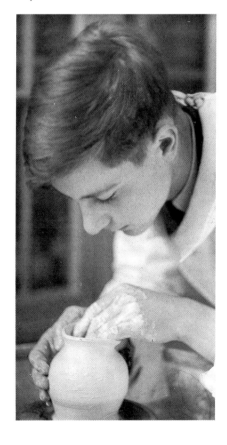

Walton's efforts to raise standards through the classics also inspired achievement in other areas of study. Boys entering the sixth form but not selected for the classical elite shone in history, modern languages and science. These subjects accounted for fourteen of the twenty-four Oxbridge awards gained by UCS boys between 1945 and 1954, classics accounting for the remaining ten. In 1954 the 207 boys in the sixth form were divided between classics, history and modern languages (103), science (99) and arts (5). The inspectors visiting the school that year concluded that attempts were being made in the sixth form to provide the broader education for the most able that had been neglected previously. They felt that modern languages and science appeared not to suffer; but some boys, in retrospect, regretted that their scientific knowledge in particular was deficient. Others too, who stubbornly refused to take classics, resented Walton's dismissive attitude towards them.

The inspectors were more critical of some of the more eccentric features of the curriculum. For some reason successive headmasters had placed greater importance on houses and forms than departments. This weakness had shown up repeatedly in previous generations, and in 1954 the inspection report once again noted that 'it is an unusual feature of the school that departmental organisation hardly exists except in science'. They also found that English throughout the school was taught only sparingly up to fifth form and there was not a single English specialist on the staff. While the inspectors felt that 'the less able boys seem to be sympathetically handled, to work hard and avoid the feeling that they are failures or people of inferior value', boys in the lowest ability stream were entered for as few as four O levels, which only one-third of them passed. One wonders what happened to the other two-thirds, especially since there was little careers advice at the school. But this was not an unusual situation among the more select academic schools in the 1950s.

Pastoral care within the school under Walton was based primarily not on the Demes, which, like Eve's original houses, organised sporting and other corporate activities, but on the forms, where the same master took his form through from entry to O level. Aubrey Morley, both form master and Deme warden, felt that responsibility was shared, with much information on pastoral matters exchanged and discussions held in the common room. The inspection team in 1954 was impressed to discover that 'the responsibility for good and sensible behaviour rests squarely on the individual', a characteristic boys from previous generations would have recognised. Although corporal punishment had been reintroduced by Kendall and was used from time to time by Walton, he preferred other ways of drawing the implications of their misdemeanours to the boys' attention. When a few boys set up a poker school, news reached Walton. They were surprised when one evening the headmaster breezed into the classroom, sat down and observed the boys in session,

Serious work in the science laboratory.

making the occasionally informed comment on their play. When the game had been completed, he got up to go and, almost incidentally, asked them if they knew they were breaking school rules. He suggested that they should come to his study every Friday with a profit and loss account of the week's activities. This was enough for the poker school to peter out, brought to an end by gentle deflation, without rancour or resentment. An equally unorthodox approach to tackling gambling was the hymn pools, where boys were encouraged to bet a few pennies on which hymn would next be sung in assembly. Walton's intention was to demonstrate the risks of gambling, that losses would always outweigh gains. But it was misunderstood – an article appeared in a national newspaper and at least one parent complained. The boys, though, were never much excited about which hymn might come up each day and thought, in Richard Pike's words, that it was just 'another of Fruity's weird ideas'.

The inspectors concluded in 1954 that 'the school provided all that one requires for intelligent, sensitive, straightforward citizens'. Among the citizens emerging from Walton's UCS were future leading academics, college heads and national museum curators, mountaineers, lyricists and businessmen. The boys, the inspectors wrote, were 'conspicuously easy and at home in their relations with adults', but the inspectors, like many outside observers of the school before and since, seemed perplexed how this happy state of affairs could be achieved, despite the fact, as they remarked, that the boys were 'rather apt not to display at school those positive refinements of good manners which have to be continuously practised'. When the inspectors met with members of Council and the headmaster at the end of the inspection, they suggested in relation to the boys that perhaps 'forthrightness often didn't stop to think'. The chairman of Council, Sir Malcolm Hilbery, a former pupil and an eminent judge, riposted that 'forthrightness is one of the best results of the education here'. Walton added that he thought in their openness and self-confidence 'the boys were like north-country boys', to which the chief inspector added that this was so, except that at UCS 'they talk more easily'.

BELOW: School posters from the 1950s by (LEFT) J.R. Booth and (RIGHT) M.J. Rhodes.

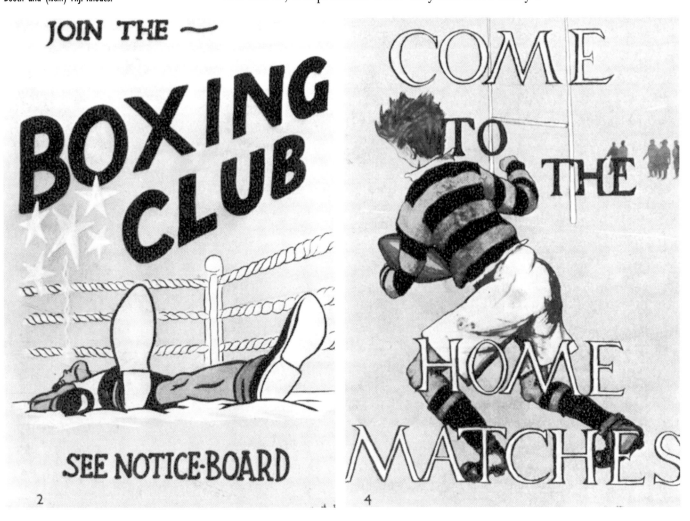

Walton's influence on UCS was undeniable. The inspection report noted: 'the whole school is now so clearly the expression of his decided views on the bringing up of boys'. Walton believed that one of the great merits of UCS as a day school was 'that the personality of boys is developed by, and their unity of spirit consists in, diversity of opinion'. He encouraged the individuality so long fostered by UCS. In the words of Sir Roger Bannister, the school 'made the personality of the boy the centre of what he was allowed to do, rather than trying to imprint on the boy some pattern that the school had determined'. One former pupil recalled that from the moment a boy entered the school, he was 'made to feel he is someone who matters'.

Underlying all this was Walton's deeply felt, but largely concealed, Christian faith. The most conspicuous sign of this as far as the boys were concerned came through those instances in assembly when Walton translated with fervour passages from the Greek New Testament. Unlike Kendall, Walton never had any qualms about using the New Testament during assemblies. The large number of Jewish boys, in the true UCS spirit of tolerance, took this in their stride, just as they did the annual carol services that Walton introduced. But when Arthur Eedle and his friends gathered at the end of the summer term in 1950 for the usual talk Walton gave to leavers, they were astounded by his parting words: 'Finally I commend you to Christ without whom you can never find real purpose or peace in life'. Eedle wrote: 'I was stunned. I can hear him saying it now, after the passage of some 55 years. We all looked at each other across the room, utterly bewildered'. It was part of the hidden Walton few people ever saw.

Boys often found Walton unsettling. While he seemed to prefer the company of boys to that of most of his staff, Walton sometimes strove too hard to achieve the rapport he desired, making them feel uneasy. Upsetting one senior boy on his last day by insensitively telling a story against him, he later realised his error and ended up shepherding the boy around the playground, his arm round his shoulder, making his apologies and trying to explain why he had used the story. Most unsettling of all, perhaps, was what Richard Pike has called Walton's 'sublimated prurience'. Walton appears to have been a sexual innocent. One Old Gower recalled with disapproval instances where Walton kissed boys, but one assumes that if this was openly done, it was innocent in intention. Others recall boys being taken to Walton's home, but this too appears to have been done openly, and, of course, he did live with his sister. But he seems to have felt that broaching matters of sex was one way of deepening his relationship with some of the boys. In his sixth-form classics classes this took the form of choosing the most sexually graphic texts for discussion, which he explained with a knowing coyness that had most boys shrinking in their seats with embarrassment.

Viewing art in the South Block Gallery, 1953.

Poster by C.B. Huntley.

93

THIS AND FACING PAGE: More school posters from the 1950s by (ABOVE) D. Winter.

BELOW: 'Bring what you can for auction', by P.B. Townsend.

Nevertheless, Pike's conclusion was one shared by most boys who knew Walton as their headmaster: 'You felt he knew you, accepted you and appreciated your individuality. He inspired affection in us and returned it in a non-physical way by teasing or laughter. He was on our side'.

Walton's achievements were secured at huge personal cost. He was overworked, had few close friends and antagonised his colleagues unnecessarily. His inability to delegate, his obsessive determination to control every area of the school – often to the considerable irritation of his staff – and his unremitting ambition to win excellence through change, all increased the pressure on him. He burdened himself even further by judging any progress made by the school only from the date of his own arrival, showing a lofty disregard for the contribution made by his predecessors to the underlying ethos of the school. Keeping his highly-strung, thoroughbred temperament in check demanded immense self-control, and eventually the burdens and expectations he imposed upon himself took their toll.

There were signs of this decline. Walton had always been concerned about the loss of school keys, but he became increasingly obsessed about this threat to security. On one occasion a boy had managed to obtain a master key to the classrooms and locked them all (with their occupants inside) shortly before assembly, resulting in an almost empty great hall. (This came shortly after the same boy had changed the recorded carillon in the parish church to play 'Cigarettes, whisky and wild, wild women' on April Fool's Day.) Walton declared that staff losing their keys would lose a year's increment from their salary. The craft master, Mr Stephenson, almost immediately mislaid his key and duly reported the fact. There are two versions of the consequences. The first, recorded by Ivor Wilkinson, tells of Walton publicly humiliating Stephenson by posting a notice declaring the salary deduction on the board in the common room. Viewed with resignation by those who had seen such behaviour before, newer members of staff were appalled. The second version, from other members of the common room at that time, suggests that Walton felt unable to impose the declared penalty. In any event, it was a salutary warning for staff.

Then there were his ever-increasing demands on others, boys and staff, which led him to change the grades for performance reported in school reports. On a scale from 'a' to 'e', he reclassified 'c' as 'competent', 'd' as 'below competence' and 'e' as 'valueless'. Some also felt that Walton was allowing his Christian fervour to show through at the expense of the school's traditional tolerance. Ivor Wilkinson notes that some Old Gowers were concerned, on the one hand, that too many new boys were blond and blue-eyed and, on the other, that Jewish boys were too often faced with only ham at lunchtime.

One senior boy, in conversation with Walton during his last year, was surprised to hear the head confide in him that the only two people he trusted at UCS were David Black-Hawkins and the school's plumber. Given Walton's record for undermining, often openly, sometimes secretively, even those picked out as his closest allies, perhaps this was scarcely surprising.

In any event, Walton was absent from school through ill-health for the second half of the summer term in 1955. It is assumed he had a nervous breakdown. While he was in hospital, his sister had a serious fall in the gardens at the school and later died from complications caused by her injuries. Towards the end of the autumn term Walton was again away from school for two weeks, returning just before the end of term. On the last day of term he was highly agitated, warning the wardens he feared the boys might cause a disturbance during the Christmas concert. Nothing happened. When Geoffrey Carrick met Walton afterwards and remarked on how smoothly everything had gone, Walton simply asked, 'Do you think we've got them cowed?'

In December 1955, on the night of the last day of term, while the school dance was being held, Cecil Walton went home to his house in Arkwright Road and hanged himself from the banisters. It was his second attempt at suicide. Two days previously he had taken an overdose of tablets and had been unconscious for two hours before recovering. His entire estate, worth £45,000 (nearly £800,000 today), went to Teddy Vogel. Walton was only fifty years old. A reverential tribute from a former school captain, P.B. Townsend, in *The Times* in January 1956 concluded that, thanks to Walton, many boys left UCS 'with a capacity to ask the right questions about themselves and about society and a capacity to initiate change and manage things'.

Within the school there was no public reference to the manner of Walton's death, although the fact of his suicide was quietly made known. Those most shocked by the manner of his death were perhaps those who had heard him commit them to Christ. The notice of Walton's death in the school magazine noted that a man who worked too hard and had almost no other interests would find it hard to forgive himself for failing to give all he had to the school, just as he found it hard to forgive others for the same weakness. The school paid homage and then moved on. Walton had achieved a great deal during his time at UCS. His legacy would turn out to be both a blessing and a curse.

Top: Poster by B.R. Bryan.

Above: 'Mirror Making' by D. McLeish.

95

'Tolerance and independence'

1956–1978

Walton had appointed David Black-Hawkins, the only member of staff he professed to trust, as vice-master in 1952. In Walton's absence, Black-Hawkins had acted as head during the summer of 1955, at a time, as Geoffrey Carrick later recalled, when 'there was some uncertainty within the school and a measure of discontent among the staff'. He impressed many with his combination of firmness and tact, qualities sorely needed in the term after Walton's death. He was also regarded with the utmost respect by both boys and staff. Council appreciated the need for continuity and consolidation after the tension and unpredictability of the Walton years. In David Black-Hawkins they saw the man

School grounds, 1970s.

they wanted. His appointment in the spring of 1956, aged forty, was different in several ways. He was the first and only headmaster of UCS to be appointed from the common room, and the first not to have a classics degree. It had also been some considerable time since a headmaster had come to the role as a married man. His wife Ruth, a remarkable woman in her own right, gave him invaluable support.

David Black-Hawkins had been educated at Wellington College and Corpus Christi, Cambridge, where he gained a first-class honours degree in French and German. At UCS he quickly gained a reputation for the breadth and depth of learning he imparted to senior boys and for the engrossing manner in which he did so. Originally intended for a military career, he served in the Second World War with the Intelligence Corps in the Middle East and at Bletchley Park. A tall, imposing figure, always immaculately dressed, he had style and flair. An outstanding public speaker, he was courteous and cultured, affable and good-humoured. Boys were in awe of this urbane and patrician figure, growing to respect him as they became more senior. As far as staff were concerned, there could hardly have been a greater contrast with his predecessor. As Geoffrey Carrick tellingly recorded, 'Whatever disagreements there may have been, his staff looked on him as a good and loyal friend. They always knew that he would back them up, that their talents would be supported and that privileged knowledge would never be leaked'. Black-Hawkins may have seemed imperious, but he was no autocrat in the Walton mould. He preferred, said Carrick, 'to be a feudal monarch, a *primus inter pares*, directing and guiding the turbulent barons on his staff with persuasion, tact and understanding'. The new headmaster seemed to possess all the attributes necessary to act as the safety valve for the pent-up steam that had to be let off post-Walton, while gently perpetuating Walton's legacy.

Black-Hawkins was keenly aware that UCS was based on a strong liberal tradition developed by each headmaster in turn, perpetuated by an able and cultured staff attracted by the school's atmosphere of tolerance and understanding. During his tenure he would have the benefit of talented teachers such as Jim Darlaston and Denis Lester, Ian McGregor and Neville Ireland, Terry Morris and John Hubbard, some of whom had joined the school with him, others whom he appointed himself. This combination of existing staff and new appointments helped to make the common room at UCS as warm and welcoming for newcomers as the head himself had found it when he joined the School.

UCS boys, as Black-Hawkins later described them, remained 'direct, self-respecting and in many cases independent-minded … we bring them up to think for themselves and if they sometimes seem self-opinionated, that is not altogether to be wondered at'. Others continued to be puzzled by this at times:

David Black-Hawkins, headmaster 1956–75.

Societies and Clubs flourished, *The Gower*, 1958.

when the headmaster announced at speech day in 1960 that the school day was being extended, it prompted a spontaneous outburst of booing and hissing from the boys, provoking loud applause from parents and other guests in an embarrassed attempt to cover up this disconcerting behaviour.

The more obvious aspects of UCS's liberal stance included continuing to welcome refugees from oppression, with a second-year Hungarian boy joining the school, having left his home country after the Russian invasion in 1956; and a wide variety of badges – usually banning the bomb – sported by boys in the early 1960s. There was, as in so many schools, criticism of the lack of interest shown by boys in school societies, which was attributed, perhaps unfairly, to a laissez-faire attitude.

A vigorous defence of the school's approach was given in an editorial written by boys in the April 1963 edition of the school magazine. The article stressed that liberalism at UCS was not the same as 'anything goes' – any boy overstepping the mark into antisocial behaviour had to be turned back. While UCS 'prefers to leave behaviour to each person's common sense', and believed in 'the importance of the individual in the community and to treat his problems on their own merits', each boy also had obligations towards his peers. This was the line stressed by David Black-Hawkins: 'Although at UCS tolerance and independence were especially cultivated, this was not to the point of laxity or eccentricity'.

Black-Hawkins later admitted that his approach to the role of headmaster had been influenced by Walton's mistakes. 'My predecessor, one of the ablest men I have ever met, achieved a marvellous degree of efficiency by regulating every detail of school life himself, but in the process he went far to destroy initiative in his staff and at inadmissible cost to himself.' Black-Hawkins, like Kendall, preferred to delegate as much as possible to his staff. He helped to liberate talents suppressed or ignored by Walton, creating a much freer atmosphere within the school, accompanied by a sense of opportunity. In the words of one master, staff 'smiled again … they began to give again of their generosity and talents'.

Black-Hawkins did much to foster the arts in their broadest sense at UCS. During his first year, school drama was officially revived. A steady stream of productions, classical and modern, flowed every succeeding year under the direction of such as like Ian McGregor and Colin Holloway. The boys formed a Theatre Club, organising visits to the latest productions, and pupils wrote, directed and performed their own plays. The choral society continued the annual performance of major works, such as Bach's *St John Passion* or *Mass in B Minor*, suitably tailored by Harold Flook to the talents available within UCS. Joint concerts with the girls from South Hampstead High School began again in 1962, reviving long-lapsed links.

Harold Flook conducted the Choral Society. Colin Myles wrote of his remarkable achievement: 'It was said by many, "The Choral Society changed my life"' and Black-Hawkins observed: 'But primarily he made it all such fun; with his gentle mockery and calculated ingenuousness, he jollied along the boys of UCS, the girls of South Hampstead and a large band of friends of the school and parents who came back each year long after their sons had departed. They knew him to be an expert and appreciated his unassuming modesty, the boys … quite simply loved him.'

Black-Hawkins encouraged drama and masters such as Colin Holloway and Ian McGregor directed theatrical productions with great enthusiasm and commitment. Below a scene from a play staged in the Crypt Theatre, 1965.

ABOVE: Dramatic Society production of *The Love of Four Colonels* by Peter Ustinov, 1969.

BELOW: Julian Lloyd-Webber attended the school in the 1960s.

One of the school's pupils in the early 1960s was Julian Lloyd-Webber, the renowned cellist. He was sent to UCS not because of its reputation for music, but because his parents believed he would have more time for playing. They were right. Lloyd-Webber already knew he wanted to play the cello professionally, in sharp contrast to most of his peers, who had given their futures little thought. Lloyd-Webber was tentative when he arrived, thinking other boys might find his obsession funny or odd. Instead, he later reflected, 'I found them very tolerant on the whole'. He discovered that music was encouraged at UCS, although 'there wasn't actually, at that time, much music in the school itself – not really very much at all. There was an orchestra but it was hardly something that you'd say the school was strong at'.

Nevertheless, although orchestral performance was not a central part of musical activity at UCS in the 1960s, small-scale performances were fostered during that decade, by Jack Davis in particular. A fine oboist, and a graduate of the Royal Academy of Music, he employed his musical talents at UCS by developing a fine chamber choir, which tackled with success works from Palestrina to Maxwell Davies. When he left, he worked in Africa for some years, inspiring one young African, Robert Kamasaka, to receive his education at UCS. After studying at university in the UK, Kamasaka eventually returned to Uganda, where he founded the Equatorial College School

(ECS). This owed much to the influence of UCS, which today takes a close interest in and provides practical support for ECS.

The scale of musical provision at UCS changed two years after Lloyd-Webber left the school, with the arrival of Colin Myles as the school's first director of music in 1969. Myles, a vivacious conductor, introduced generations of boys to many great works during his stay, which lasted until 2001. His extensive musical knowledge rubbed off on both boys and staff. In 1971 Harold Flook finally handed over his choral society responsibilities, having kept the musical muse alive at UCS for a quarter of a century.

The revival and encouragement of drama and music exemplified the way in which UCS began to enjoy those broader activities already available at many other schools. One of the more unusual during the 1960s and 1970s was the car maintenance course and the motoring club run by John Hubbard. The club, with its own old Austin A35, provided many boys with their first driving lessons, using the school playground after games on two afternoons a week.

Cellists during orchestra practice.

Colin Myles was director of music from 1969 until his retirement in 2001. His deep love for his subject was inspirational to many and his outstanding contribution to the musical life of the School endures today.

Soccer was introduced to the School by Robin Jenks and Mike Alsford in the late 1960s.

Denis Lester, as well as pouring his time into the school boat club, introduced French exchange visits and revived the overseas trips he had first begun in the 1930s. In 1962 there were excursions to Greece and Denmark, and in 1964, the year of Lester's retirement, to France. These continued on a haphazard basis, ranging from skiing trips to Austria to cruises off West Africa. Encouraged by this example (and the long tradition established by the Old Gowers) the school rugby team went to France on its first overseas tour in 1964, and repeated the experience in 1968 and again in 1972.

Lester was president of the boat club for three years from 1959. The club, under Hugh Cowham until 1958 and Geoffrey Page from 1959 onwards, was in its heyday. During the 1958 season, for instance, the school put at least twelve racing eights on the river. Under Page, an accomplished oarsman, the school's 1st IV represented Great Britain at the World Youth Championships in 1967 and 1972, and the 1st VIII represented England in the Home Countries race against Scotland in 1971, winning by six lengths. This success became much more difficult to maintain after the loss of the school's boathouse in 1971.

New sports were introduced, such as softball, although they were often short-lived, and others were reintroduced, most notably soccer and hockey in 1968. It was the reintroduction of soccer which made the most impact, the first major change in sport at the school for some years and one that was hugely popular. Two new masters, Robin Jenks and Mike Alsford, joining the school in 1967, were both keen soccer players. They felt soccer was the ideal sport to rejuvenate the barren spring term sporting calendar. Such an idea, even in soccer-mad north-west London, was regarded at UCS as heretical by traditionalists and diehard rugby players. But with the diplomatic advice and

Coxed four training at Henley, 1972. This crew won the National Junior Championships and went on to represent Great Britain in the World Youth Championships.

ABOVE LEFT: Sponsored walk for Oxfam, 1968.

RIGHT: Voluntary Service activities included helping a boy learn English ...

help of Colin Boothroyd, a senior master, soccer was introduced in 1968 as an unofficial option. In 1970, after 'much battling', to use Alsford's phrase, soccer became an official spring term choice. Under Colin Boothroyd, the school tennis team won the Glanville Cup in 1967 and the Youll Cup in 1972.

One of the most striking reconnections during David Black-Hawkins' time was with voluntary work. The school under Walton had lost touch with the Docklands Settlement, which, although links were renewed in 1957, was becoming an anachronism in more prosperous times. A few years later, in 1965, the Voluntary Service scheme was started through the initiative of Anton Barber, senior language master at the time. Boys visited elderly people, took them Christmas parcels and supplied them with winter firewood, worked on an adventure playground, helped in hospitals, assisted the disabled and ran a weekly girls' club for disadvantaged youngsters. In 1967 and 1968 boys took part in sponsored walks for Oxfam. The latter event, involving more than 2000 children in the London area, was organised by a UCS sixth-former, Giles Pegram. In the early 1970s the sixth-form committee organised fund-raising involving 300 pupils from several Camden schools for a charity, Outset, working with the homeless, alcoholics and drug addicts.

Black-Hawkins was also responsible for making the appointment that revitalised the Junior Branch at Holly Hill. Teddy Vogel had retired in 1962 and was followed by Michael Benson, whose tenure lasted only five years.

BELOW: ... as well as chopping firewood for the elderly.

Opportunities for tennis and fencing expanded in the 1970s.

Ian McGregor, headmaster of Holly Hill, 1967–91.

The key appointment made by Black-Hawkins was to follow Benson with Ian McGregor, who had spent three years as Black-Hawkins Deme warden. His enthusiasm breathed new life into Holly Hill. With his wife Edna, he determined that the family atmosphere for so long characteristic of Holly Hill should be conserved, but he was also committed to widening the opportunities available for Holly Hill boys. More French and science were taught, while sport was expanded to encompass football and opportunities for hockey, tennis and fencing. Key men in the development of games were Brian Duggan, with his background in hockey, cross-country and swimming, and Bill Jones, a young MCC professional. McGregor blew away the cobwebs which had settled on the life of the school since, or even before, the war. School caps disappeared; school monitors were replaced with a system that gave more boys more responsibility; and a Parents' Guild was established to create closer links with the school. He also made a start on remedying the long-term neglect of the school's physical fabric. This began with a long overdue new science block in the playground, although McGregor would have to wait patiently for another decade before more much-needed physical improvements were made. In everything he did he enjoyed the support of the school's long-serving staff, such as Eric Marston, Michael Dean, John Marshall, Jean Sladdin and Barbara Hendrie, whose sterling work inside and outside the classroom produced many boys who went on to make their mark at the senior school and beyond. Many Old Gowers will remember specifically Joanna Wormald, appointed by Michalel Benson in January 1966 and the bedrock of the school office until April 2007.

Black-Hawkins carefully dismantled the academic hothouse erected by his predecessor. With the enthusiastic and committed support of staff, he replaced it, over twenty years, with a curriculum intended to provide every boy with the much broader, more rounded education that was more in keeping with the aims of most former UCS heads. Specialisation before boys reached transitus was abandoned, as was the system of streaming that had seen some boys race to their O levels in two years. This was replaced by a three-year course followed by every boy. The end of the fast stream also brought an end to the fourth sixth-form year, with sixth-formers who were studying for Oxbridge scholarships taking their scholarship examinations during the first term of their third year and leaving school at Christmas.

All boys were now taught science subjects during their first two years in the school. Of the two subjects notoriously neglected by Walton, history became compulsory, while geography was much more widely taught. By the 1970s, Greek and Latin, compulsory in the 1950s, had become optional subjects. Some of these changes, of course, came in response to external pressures. The requirement from more and more universities for three rather than two A levels broke down the previously rigid system where, for instance, boys intending to study the arts were expected to take only arts subjects.

Staff themselves were keen to break out of Walton's academic straitjacket and offer boys more choice. David Black-Hawkins was always receptive to their suggestions, giving them every consideration and encouragement.

Bill Jones, the only teacher to teach boys from the ages of 7 to 18, pictured here with Junior rugby.

BELOW, LEFT TO RIGHT: School life: science class; art class with Maurice Johnson, head of art; working in the control box.

ABOVE: Most Old Gowers remember the cross-country training on Hampstead Heath, 1968.

BELOW: Cricket nets in the school grounds.

BOTTOM: Conferring during a match.

Initially this meant that some staff would teach several subjects. Ian McGregor, for example, had taught not only history in the sixth form, but also English, and briefly, because two boys expressed a wish to go to the London School of Economics, a course in economics and government studies. Gradually more specialists were recruited for this expanded field. So while John Usher and Aubrey Morley continued to excel in their teaching of classics, for example, Adrian Runswick and those who followed him brought an equally high standard to the teaching of English.

It is difficult to assess the impact of all this on the school's academic record. But there was a steady increase in the number of boys taking up university places. By 1964, when seventeen boys left for Oxbridge, university accounted for more than 60 per cent of sixth-form leavers. In 1969 the school achieved a record number of open award winners to Oxbridge, with thirteen boys in a variety of subjects. In 1975, the last year of the Black-Hawkins headship, over 70 per cent of boys were leaving for university, with a further seventeen entering either Oxford or Cambridge. That was probably the last year for boys who had come to UCS on a scholarship from Middlesex County Council, the scheme finally coming to an end in the late 1960s.

All this helped the school to tread a fine line between order and chaos during the social upheavals of the 1960s. Black-Hawkins confessed that sometimes he found this difficult to achieve. Some boys felt that the school did not keep up with the times. Martin Lewis, the producer, was at UCS in the early 1960s and hated his school days. His education was too academic, too uninteresting, unconnected to what was happening outside the King Edward VII Gates. But things did change at UCS; the question was whether they changed enough or in the right way. Hugh Dennis, a pupil from 1973 to 1980, remembered that by the mid-1970s staff were wearing bell-bottom trousers, while the boys were in patchwork jeans; UCS was 'easygoing' and 'no-one made you do anything'. The head lamented that some boys were calling some staff by their first names. John Hubbard, who joined the school in 1966, at first bemused to find how much pupils and staff were at ease with each other, discovered that the boys 'could interact almost as equals and the relationship wasn't abused by pupils or staff'. The whole ethos of UCS was still something of a mystery to those on the outside. Hubbard and his fellow member of staff Robin Jenks took a cricket team of long-haired boys to King's College School (KCS), Wimbledon, in the early 1970s. As Jenks and his colleague from KCS followed the UCS team on to the field in their umpires' coats, the latter remarked to Jenks, 'I see you have the same problem as we do'. He was perplexed to hear from Jenks that long hair simply was not seen as a problem at UCS.

With greater responsibilities given to young people, including the reduction in the age of majority to eighteen in 1967, the feeling grew among senior boys at UCS that their status within the school was not sufficiently recognised. In particular, there was no dedicated sixth-form area within the school – at least, not a space that was considered suitable. The lack of sixth-form facilities, which senior members of the staff pressed the head to remedy, was only one example of how far UCS was falling behind other schools. An appeal in 1957 had raised the funds to provide a new library, laboratory and music room, and to purchase a house for the headmaster, but by 1970 the library and music room were already inadequate, while all the laboratories were crying out for improvements. John Hubbard found the place 'quaint and run down', and was astonished to find that the two chemistry laboratories had been largely untouched since the opening of the school. The shabbiness in many respects hid a brilliance, not just in the science departments, but elsewhere in the school, although some said that the heavy oak doors of the classrooms around the great hall in some instances shielded from view teaching methods as unchanged as the physical surroundings.

The school woke up to the need for action at the end of the 1960s. The ultimate proposal was to create a sixth-form centre and a purpose-built theatre and music rooms. An appeal raised £170,000 (£1.4 million today) and the Duke of Kent opened the completed building, named Kents with his consent, on 22 May 1974. Money left over allowed the swimming pool to be heated and given a roof – no more would the school magazine have to report, as it did in 1972, that the water had been too cold for any serious competitive swimming

Top: The foundation stone for the Sixth Form Centre was laid in 1973 by Sir Norman Kipping. Lord Lloyd of Hampstead, John Neal (Council member and school surveyor) and Sir Norman Kipping, chairman of governors, who later handed over to Lord Lloyd.

Above: Opening of the Sixth Form Centre by the Duke of Kent, 22 May 1974. Sir Norman Kipping welcoming the Duke of Kent.

Below left: The sixth form centre. Right: Inside the centre.

University College School
Theatre Frognal Hampstead N.W.3
CONCERT
AL CASEY
FRANZ JACKSON
MIKE CARR TRIO
Thursday 13th MAY 1982 7.45pm.
In advance £1·50
At the door £2·00

David Lund organised the first jazz concert in 1975. Since then the School has welcomed numerous jazz musicians and raised large amounts for charity. TOP LEFT: Poster for concert; RIGHT: Famous jazz musicians at the School with David Lund, second from right. From left: Lennie Bush, Adelaide Carr, Alan Clare, David Lund and Tony Crombie; ABOVE: The Humphrey Lyttelton Band.

Drama rehearsal, 1974.

to take place. At the same time the laboratories were at last upgraded. It was not enough – the headmaster expressed his regret that a planned programme of maintenance, refurbishment and redecoration had never been achieved – but it was a start.

The creation of a sixth-form centre brought reform to the way in which the sixth form was run. Boys elected their own committee, guided by three sixth-form tutors, appointed from senior members of staff. The theatre, known as the New Theatre, quickly became not just a vital part of school life, but also one of the most visible signs of the links between UCS and the local community. David Lund, who taught English at the school, organised a jazz concert on 6 March 1975, with the English jazz pianist Eddie Thompson and his trio. Among the jazz stars who followed in Thompson's footsteps to UCS over the next thirty years were James Moody, Bud Shank, Al Haig, Ruby Braff, Jay McShane, Ray Bryant, Adelaide Hall and Blossom Dearie. Fellow jazz musicians would often come to hear their peers – the Modern Jazz Quartet once dropped in to listen to Eddie 'Lockjaw' Davis. Sound and lighting were the responsibility of successive generations of boys and each concert raised money for charity. This was only one of the ways in which the theatre became so important to the school, hosting a wide range of events.

David Black-Hawkins retired at the end of the summer term in 1975. He had been a loyal servant of the school, steadying its course in the wake of Cecil Walton. Change had been gentle and gradual, placing more emphasis on a broader education for every boy, without losing sight of Walton's goals. He had succeeded in renewing the relationship between staff and head which had essentially broken down. Like all his predecessors, he had ensured that the school's distinctive nature endured. For Black-Hawkins, this was quite an achievement during a time of turbulent social change. If standards of outward appearances, in particular, had been allowed to slip, this was almost understandable, as long as beneath the surface those characteristics still survived which enabled boys of all backgrounds and aptitudes to thrive at UCS.

Black-Hawkins should also be praised for reversing the autocracy created under Walton and enabling the much fuller participation of staff within the school. Perhaps, as is often the case, the pendulum swung too far in the other direction and too much freedom was given to staff without proper accountability. This situation was not unique to UCS. But it was compounded by the feeling, expressed by one member of staff, that 'we were our own market and "special", a Waltonian conceit with less and less to substantiate it'. One result of this was to insulate UCS and its long-serving pool of staff from educational initiatives being taken elsewhere. The impact was most evident in the physical development of the school. It was partly why the creation of the sixth-form centre came relatively late and why so little else was done to improve the school's physical facilities. While, again, UCS was not alone in this, it lagged behind those schools which had been raising funds and putting up and equipping new buildings during the late 1960s and early 1970s.

Staff photo, taken to mark David Black-Hawkins' retirement, 1975. Back row from left: Lawrence Impey, David Lund, Mike McKeon, Ronnie Landau, Geoffrey Dicks, Terry Morris, Harry Sargent, Paul Cattermole, Robin Jenks, John Older, Hugh Pountney, Neville Ireland, Geoffrey Creber. Middle row: Colin Myles, Geoffrey Page, John Hubbard, John Couper, Nigel Yates, Alan Privett, Jack Watson, Tony Ford, Mike Alsford, Anton Barber, Ken Wooton, Steve Wells, Tony Roberts. Front row: Colin Boothroyd, Guy Hunt, Harold Flook, Peter Underwood, Aubrey Morley, Geoffrey Carrick, David Black-Hawkins, Colin Holloway, 'Bill' Glover, Paul Romage, John Usher, Tony Lewis, Cyril Wheeler (Bursar), Bob Lees.

Alan Barker, headmaster 1975–82.

Sixth-form boys, 1975.

In September 1975 UCS welcomed a new headmaster. Alan Barker was an experienced head when he arrived in Frognal. Educated at Rossall School, he studied history at Jesus College, Cambridge. After war service, when he received serious injuries, he took up teaching, first with the Workers' Educational Association, followed by a brief spell at Eton, then a period as a fellow and director of studies in history at Queen's College, Cambridge. He returned to Eton, where he remained until his appointment at the age of thirty-five as head of The Leys, the Methodist-influenced boarding school in Cambridge. Here he spent the next seventeen years. He and his wife became deeply involved in local politics, serving as Conservative councillors. This was the start of a political career which would see Jean Barker join the House of Lords as a Conservative peer under the name of Baroness Trumpington in 1980.

Times had changed since David Black-Hawkins had broken the tradition of appointing classicists to the UCS headship, so it was not unusual that the new headmaster should have a degree in history. What was unusual was that Alan Barker was in his early fifties – the oldest appointment made by the school – after a teaching career spent entirely in boarding schools. It is said that the appointment was made because someone entirely different, experienced and reputable was needed to reinvigorate the school. But, as one Old

Rugby.

Gower and Council member put it, Barker, 'with experience only of boarding schools, of common rooms which followed the head, without any experience of living in the cockpit of London day schools, was out of his depth'. Barker's autocratic instincts clashed with the way in which the common room had developed an almost democratic alliance with the head during the latter years of Black-Hawkins. Some said that the balance of power had altered too much in favour of the common room, but whatever the truth of the matter, there was a lack of mutual trust and tolerance between the two sides, which made difficult any agreement on changes the head might have wished to introduce. Although one of his first acts was to create an organisation to channel parental involvement into the school, the Parents' Guild, he found it hard to relate to the metropolitan background of UCS parents and sometimes found it difficult to conceal his impatience with them. A flavour of his trenchant views came at speech day in 1981, when he criticised a certain type of parent: 'Divorce, too much money, too many expectations, too little concern with the school (simply using it as a convenience), parents never coming to support their sons in school activities, creates a boy who is not civilised'. Barker tried hard to understand what made UCS work, but found himself at the end of a long queue of outsiders who confessed to being completely baffled.

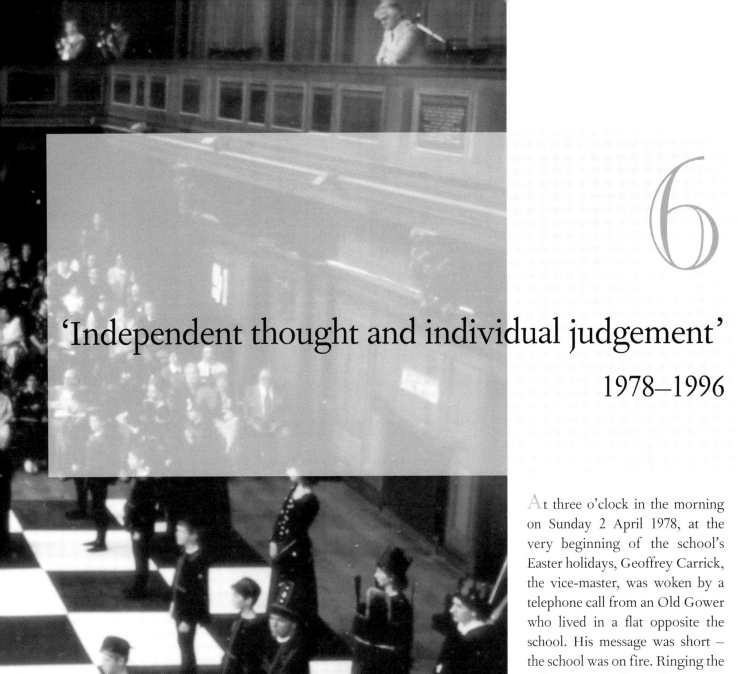

6

'Independent thought and individual judgement'

1978–1996

At three o'clock in the morning on Sunday 2 April 1978, at the very beginning of the school's Easter holidays, Geoffrey Carrick, the vice-master, was woken by a telephone call from an Old Gower who lived in a flat opposite the school. His message was short – the school was on fire. Ringing the police to confirm the news, Carrick came down to the school to find the roof ablaze and firemen already working hard to put out the flames. When John Couper, the head of English, arrived at Frognal, staff, parents and pupils were looking on aghast at the destruction. 'My study was in the basement under the hall', he later recalled, 'and when I could get to it, all my books were in ruins from the firemen's hoses, and the smell of burnt wood hung around the school for months.'

Living chess in the great hall, 1970s.

The fire destroyed the great hall. The loss of the physical focus of the school brought home to many staff and boys how much UCS meant to them. The classrooms surrounding the hall were severely damaged. The cause of the fire was established as arson, although the perpetrator was never caught. Once the building had been made safe, it was possible for parents, staff and boys to help each other in retrieving what they could.

There was a fortnight to go before the school was due to reopen. Alan Barker rose to the challenge and united the staff behind him. He was in his element as he dealt with all the details necessary to provide temporary teaching accommodation and began the task of planning the reconstruction of the devastated building. He received invaluable advice and assistance from the bursar, Michael White, the vice-master, Geoffrey Carrick, and three members of Council, Eric Beverley, Ian King and John Neal. In one sense, the school had been lucky. Only the hall and surrounding classrooms had been affected. The school office, gym, laboratories and refectory were untouched. Twenty-two temporary classrooms were installed at the back of the school, on the tennis courts and along the top of the garden, allowing UCS to reopen, on time, on 17 April. The first phase of recovery had been completed.

The damage was amply covered by the school's fire insurance. The Parents' Guild opened the Phoenix Fund to raise money for contingencies. It was decided that as well as faithfully recreating the great hall, the opportunity would be taken to upgrade the classrooms and redevelop the water-damaged crypt to provide more teaching space, a careers room and other facilities. The work carried out in restoring the hall, by the contractor Bovis, was outstanding in every respect, from the ornate plaster ceiling to the wooden panelling and oak doors to the classrooms. The first assembly in the restored hall took place

Portakabins were brought in to serve as temporary classrooms.

FACING PAGE: The terrible fire of 2 April 1978 destroyed the great hall and damaged classrooms in the main building. CLOCKWISE FROM TOP LEFT: all ablaze; the burnt-out roof of the great hall; a sombre Alan Barker and Geoffrey Carrick survey the remains of the First World War memorial; surveying the damage in the great hall.

BELOW LEFT: Contractors begin work on rebuilding the School. RIGHT: Builders at work.

Neville Ireland teaching history in a Portakabin after the fire.

BELOW LEFT: Alan Barker launches with champagne the ceremony to lift the dome back onto the roof. RIGHT: Everyone stopped to watch the event.

in September 1979. It was a triumph for Alan Barker, reinforced by the formal opening of the hall by the Queen on 27 February 1980, a fitting way to mark the 150th anniversary of the founding of the school.

What were the effects of the fire? It was a personal success for the headmaster and the damage caused by the fire gave the opportunity to improve areas of the school neglected for decades. But some felt that the gap between the fire and the completion of the restoration was long enough for the school to lose, rather than regain, its sense of direction. Certainly the editors of the school magazine in the autumn of 1979 said that it would be an overstatement to claim that 'the school itself, as a corporate body, has been repaired, let alone improved'. For instance, although weekly assemblies were held in the New Theatre and relayed to the sixth-form centre above, for the rest of the week everything else took place through the Demes. At least one Deme warden felt that this emphasised a sense of dislocation and diminished the unity of the school. There was also a view that the school expended so much energy in limited reconstruction and improvement that none was left to devote to the physical expansion being pursued by so many other schools.

While so much time and energy were understandably being expended on the senior school, change was also taking place at the Junior Branch. The most noticeable changes were physical. There was a view that for too long the physical development of the Junior Branch had been overlooked by UCS. Alan Barker sympathised with this and, in association with Ian McGregor, submitted a proposal to remedy the situation. In 1978 plans were approved to create a music room, along with a new art room, library and, subsequently, staff room. Alan Barker, with his experience of The Leys, also came to UCS

wishing to introduce the Common Entrance examination for all those coming to UCS, whether or not they were from the Junior Branch. For Ian McGregor and his staff, this simply seemed to underline a feeling that the senior school lacked proper understanding of the aims and objectives pursued at Holly Hill. Throughout Holly Hill's history, boys entering the Junior Branch had always been able to move on to UCS, regardless of their attainments. The value of this was intangible, but McGregor also showed for the first time, through a statistical survey, the outstanding contribution made by most Junior Branch entrants to the senior school. The idea of Common Entrance was dropped. It had been proved, as Ian McGregor recalled, that the work of the staff at the Junior Branch had established

ABOVE, FROM LEFT: Queen Elizabeth II came in 1980 to open the newly restored School, accompanied by Eric Beverley, chairman of Council; Mike Alsford and David Bernard at the opening ceremony in 1980; Queen Elizabeth II and Alan Barker coming out of the headmaster's study, 1980.

> in the minds of young boys that quality that was to enable them to make the most of all the great things that Frognal increasingly offered. What Holly Hill achieved is an integral part of what UCS as a whole achieved at its very best, and is no coincidental subsidiary.

The effort Barker had invested in securing the future of the school after the blaze took its toll on his health. In November 1981 he suffered a major stroke from which he never really recovered. Confined to a wheelchair, he retired early in July 1982, aged only fifty-eight. He had been at UCS just over seven years, of which the fire and its consequences accounted for a third. But he had also welcomed boys to the school through the Conservative government's assisted places scheme and presided over the opening in 1982 of a design technology centre in memory of the late chairman of Council, Eric Beverley, who had died suddenly only a month after the formal reopening of the great hall.

Inside the great hall.

UCS boys at Beckford primary school, 1980.

Fun in the snow.

Geoffrey Carrick, the vice-master, took over the running of the school from the time Alan Barker fell ill until the arrival of his successor. With the assistance of his colleagues, Carrick steered the school calmly through almost a year and a half. As well as being a tribute to Carrick's own qualities, it was also due to reforms already implemented by Barker. In place was a senior management team, including the head, vice-master, head of the Junior Branch and bursar, which made continuity possible, as did Council's recently created Finance and General Purposes Committee, which had shown its worth during the aftermath of the fire. This did not necessarily make it easy for the new headmaster. When Giles Slaughter, who arrived in January 1983, heard how much was delegated to senior staff he found it difficult to understand exactly what the headmaster did.

Slaughter was forty-five years old, married to Gillian, with three daughters. Educated at the Royal Masonic School, he had read history, like his predecessor, at King's College, Cambridge. His teaching career took him to a wide variety of schools before he became headmaster of Solihull School in 1973. Solihull was an example of the schools refounded in the nineteenth century following the reform of the endowed charities. Unlike UCS, day-boys were mixed with boarders, but like UCS, the school was situated in a wealthy suburb of a major city, in this case Birmingham. Filled with energy, he had what one colleague described as an 'angular bustle'. Generous and humane, with an infectious warmth, he had a knack of making people feel involved and appreciated. The common room, initially guarded, soon grew to like their headmaster, whose habit was always to take soundings from staff before making a decision. But there was a steeliness in Slaughter's character, founded on common sense and a high regard for decency.

Slaughter found a school filled with good staff, but poorly equipped. He was appalled by the shabbiness of the buildings and the inadequacy of the facilities. The boys matched their surroundings, their untidiness jarring with the smart, dapper appearance of the head. This, he felt, was indicative of too many boys failing to achieve their potential. Driving up the standards of dress – jeans were banned, the blazer was retained – was accompanied by revising the system of reports and assessments so that improvements in outward appearances were matched by improving academic progress. Although he never got used to the scruffy dress common among UCS boys, Slaughter, like those before him, wanted to ensure they understood that freedom came with responsibilities, that attending UCS brought obligations that had to be honoured, especially the need to respect differing opinions, abilities and talents.

The headmaster did not find it easy to settle into his new post. During the first eighteen months he frequently asked himself what he was doing at UCS, but he found himself warming to the school and its distinctive way of doing things. Spending his first two terms quietly watching how the school operated, he realised that his own way of doing things, involving others, seeking opinions, being as open as possible about key issues, fitted in well with the quasi-democratic nature of the school. He began to know more and more of the boys, introducing the habit of seeing each of them on their birthday. The first time the list of birthday boys was read out in assembly, a terrible hush descended, with those named shuffling uneasily in their seats, wondering what heinous crime they had committed to send them into the presence of the headmaster.

UCS staff were a constant source of support and advice. This was a time of considerable change in the common room, with the departure during the new head's first few years of many long-serving masters. Among them were Tony Lewis, who had run the 1st XV and made geography a key subject in the curriculum. John Usher retired in 1983, after thirty-six years at the school, followed by Aubrey Morley in 1984. In the same year UCS said goodbye to John Phillips and Geoffrey Page, who both retired, as well as Neville Ireland, who moved to Loughborough Grammar School as headmaster. In 1986 Geoffrey Carrick retired, followed by Bob Lees, after thirty-five years at the school. He had been head of maths until 1973, before becoming a sixth-form tutor. Although this was an era when schools like UCS began to find it hard to recruit and then retain good staff, simply because of rocketing house prices in desirable areas of the capital, the common room always contained a core of

Giles Slaughter, headmaster 1983–1996.

talented men and women. John Couper, for instance, took over from Geoffrey Carrick as vice-master, a post he held until his retirement in 1994, when he was succeeded by Peter Underwood, who had been the first holder of the new post of director of studies. Couper and Underwood, in the tradition of Geoffrey Carrick, played invaluable supporting roles in the running of the school. Tony Roberts was a considerable English teacher and rugby player, who coached the 1st XV for many years and also ran one of the Demes. Paul Cattermole was another Deme warden, and an outstanding sports coach, who was a county cricketer, county rugby player and football league trialist. Terry Morris was an inimitable teacher of history; David Lund, also passionately interested in his pupils, was never heard to raise his voice in his English classes; John Hubbard and John Older provided inspiration in the chemistry laboratories.

Slaughter kept the Walton system of weekly meetings with senior staff, but also introduced similar meetings with heads of departments, giving them an increasing involvement in budgets and recruiting new staff. The Demes, which had developed as the principal focus for the boys' well-being, were united pastorally with the forms, reviving the role they had had under both Eve and Walton. This both eased the burden on the Deme wardens and strengthened the system of pastoral care. The head was especially keen on this

Preparing for one of the many Fun Runs organised by David Lund for charity.

Top: A watercolour of the School painted by Michael Aubrey. Bottom: Art trip to Paris, 2001.

Music at UCS. This page, clockwise from top: Junior Branch pupils practising for Speech Day; playing the tuba; the orchestra rehearses with John Bradbury at St Mary's Church, Kilburn.

Facing page: Drama productions. Main picture: *The Tempest*; Inset, left to right: *Waiting for Godot*, *Smike Mar*, Phoenix production of *Spirit of Christmas*.

TOP, MAIN PICTURE: Jon Cooke overseeing Under 11 cricket; INSET: 'Ouch!' BOTTOM LEFT: Football — James Rahamim; RIGHT: Junior rugby.

MAIN PICTURE AND INSET: Ten Tors expedition, 2004.

Expeditions play a key part in the cultural education of UCS boys. CLOCKWISE FROM TOP LEFT: Walking in Prague; Skiing in Macugnaga, Italy; Year 8 field study trip to Lanehead.

The new sports centre is a fine addition to the School, boasting facilities such as a 25m swimming pool (MAIN PICTURE); a fitness suite (INSET, MIDDLE); and a sports hall (INSET, RIGHT).

MAIN PICTURE: Speech Day, May 2007. INSET: Lord Sebastian Coe (left) was the guest speaker at the event, shown here with the headmaster Kenneth Durham (middle) and chairman of Council, Sir Victor Blank (right).

Drama productions, 1990s. ABOVE LEFT: *Jungle Rock,* 1994; TOP: *The Fosdyke Saga,* 1992; ABOVE: *Dark Side of the Moon,* 1990; BELOW: *Lord of the Flies,* 1997.

side of the school, since, as he told parents, sophisticated, streetwise north London teenagers were prey to more temptations than most. Drug abuse became an issue of growing concern. Under Slaughter, strongly supported by parents, UCS in the early 1990s was among the first schools which did not automatically expel drug offenders. The school's policy statement on the matter emphasised that boys at UCS should be regarded and treated as individuals, and while the possession, use or supply of controlled substances was not condoned, the school would do its utmost to develop a comprehensive health education programme, create an atmosphere where social issues could be discussed openly, exercising clemency where appropriate, but enforcing expulsion where necessary. There were one or two incidents, but the number of times the head himself had to take disciplinary action were limited. On one occasion when he did, he discovered, if he did not already know it, that the forthrightness and forwardness that had impressed school inspectors forty years earlier were still alive: a boy fined by the head for smoking in school blithely asked him if he took credit cards.

During the late 1980s and early 1990s UCS began to develop a range of extra-curricular activities to match those offered at other schools. Drama flourished under Mary Reade and Allan Steven, with first-class productions of such varied classics as *Guys & Dolls*, *The Crucible* and *Forty Years On*. The splendid annual choral performances continued and the school was privileged to have among its pupils one young man, Thomas Adès, who became the outstanding contemporary composer of his generation. There was another

121

Visitors to the school (FROM LEFT): Hugh Laurie, Jan Ravens and Stephen Fry, part of the cast of the Cambridge Footlights revue. The Footlights made annual visits to the Theatre; with Harold Wilson (who had two sons at the School), Mike Densham (Master 1965–80), David Lund and Alan Barker; Arthur Scargill.

Glenda Jackson with Paul Cohen.

revival of interest in school societies, numbers rising from just three in 1983 to fifteen in 1986 and thirty-four in 1991, and ranging from tiddlywinks and war games to chess and science. The shining star in this firmament was perhaps the Politics and Economics Society, which attracted a string of prominent speakers to its meetings, from Ken Livingstone, Michael Heseltine and Trevor Huddleston to three Yorkshire miners during the national strike of 1984–85. In 1986 the miners' leader, Arthur Scargill, drew a full house – 300 tickets were issued to boys on a first-come, first-served basis at 8.30 one morning and were gone within five minutes.

At speech day in 1983 the headmaster, praising the work done by UCS's Voluntary Service Unit (VSU), remarked that

a good school should complement the home and be a place where boys not only feel secure, but where they may flex their muscles and stretch their minds in meeting other young people, holding discussions with stimulating personalities, and directing into positive action their very genuine concern for the aged, the infirm, the handicapped and the lonely.

The VSU continued to raise significant funds every year for a wide variety of charities. Other fund-raising events were also held. In 1992, for instance, when the VSU raised £5750, the school as a whole raised over £20,000 for charity through bridge evenings, sponsored runs, quizzes and other activities. One of the most popular was the Miss UCS contest, when the headmaster himself judged the best drag artist of the night. The money went towards parties, outings and hampers for the elderly, and in donations to a number of local and national charities. The drawback to this fine record was that the raising of money tended to replace the active participation of pupils in projects.

One activity that had been going on for several years was the concerts for pensioners given by a group of boys and staff, which became known as the Palm Courtet. For Mike Alsford, who was involved with the Courtet for many years, this 'somehow sums up the very essence of UCS. It is hard to imagine that it could have happened at any other school'. It began after a bandleader's widow donated a collection of sheet music to the school. Alsford soon organised the Palm Court Quartet (the name was contracted to Palm Courtet as there were often more and occasionally less than four in the group) with several talented sixth-formers, giving concerts at a variety of local venues. The first annual concerts given by the group plus guests at the school began in 1979. The Courtet flourished until 1995, and in a different form the annual concerts still take place.

The wider travel horizons of young people were reflected in more ambitious and more frequent trips overseas. In 1990, for instance, the fall of the Iron Curtain encouraged visits to Romania, East Germany, Czechoslovakia,

Mike Alsford performing with the Palm Courtet.

The Palm Courtet with Mike Alsford and Lawrence Impey (Master 1974–1982) performing a Noel Coward number.

A trip to France, 1995.

Ten Tors expedition.

Yugoslavia and the Soviet Union, the last four soon to vanish from the map. Long-standing exchange links between UCS and the Lycée Marcelin Berthelot in Paris were augmented in the early 1990s, with a new relationship forged with the Collège Mendès-France in Lillebonne.

Outdoor pursuits were relatively new to UCS when Giles Slaughter became head. The stimulus to take these seriously began through the initiative of a young history teacher, Richard Palmer, who joined the school in 1978. In the following year he took the first party of UCS boys on the Ten Tors expedition. He also led parties of boys, with other members of staff, including Tony Harrison and Allan Woolley, on mountaineering trips to the Alps and the Pyrenees. Sadly, in the spring half-term of 1983, Palmer, along with a UCS pupil, David Solomons, was killed in a climbing accident in Wales. This tragedy stunned the school, and brought people closer together. Outdoor activities continued and, after considerable deliberation, the school acquired a field centre at Lanehead in Weardale, County Durham. An article in the school magazine stated: 'we will hopefully develop in our students a greater appreciation of the environment around them, and show them that there is a world north of Watford'.

Sport at UCS remained as ever just one part of the overall school activities. There had never been a win-at-all-costs approach at UCS, and indeed boys at assemblies now began to announce their sporting defeats as well as

124

triumphs. For the head, one of the principal benefits of games was the invaluable informal contact this brought between boys and staff. But sporting standards were not disregarded; the school appointed its first director of sport and several outstanding team performances were achieved. Under Allan Woolley, for instance, school cross-country teams had several successes, including the overall London Schools championship. The school's hockey and badminton sides also grew in strength, while in 1994 the soccer team, and in 1995 the 1st, 2nd and 3rd XVs, had their most successful seasons. Soccer by this time had become the most popular games option in the spring term. There were disappointments. Perhaps the greatest of these was the demise of rowing in 1990. The growing popularity of other sports, especially hockey and soccer, plus the increasing travails of the journey to the boathouse at Chiswick – making it difficult to compete with riverside schools able to take the water before morning school – led to dwindling numbers and the club was no longer viable. But proceeds from the disposal of the boats were reinvested in six dinghies for a revived sailing club, based at the more accessible reservoir at Aldenham. The other major downside of games at UCS was the desperate lack of decent indoor facilities. Plans to remedy this deficiency would form part of the head's overall strategy for improving Frognal's facilities.

Rugby.

Cross-country on Hampstead Heath on a misty morning.

125

A time capsule was buried in the school grounds in 1989. The boys chose the contents which included personal writing on topical issues such as traffic congestion in Hampstead, South Africa, Northern Ireland, the Channel Tunnel, football and the new GCSE examination as well as gifts and letters. The capsule will be dug up in 2089.

Alistair Smith, Dave Scott and John Bradbury making pizzas, Lanehead, June 1994.

The school had a good academic record when the new headmaster arrived. In his first year, UCS boys achieved twenty-three Oxbridge places, while 86 per cent of boys gained passes in their A and O level examinations. Nevertheless, Slaughter later said that he felt on his arrival that 'there were a number of boys who felt that the world owed them a living', and he was determined to ensure that in future boys appreciated that success came through effort. There will always be an argument over the standards of examinations from the 1980s onwards, as one government initiative followed another, as O levels gave way to GCSEs, with a proportion of assessed coursework – a trend later followed at higher levels, with the advent of AS levels. UCS also benefited from growing competition for places at the school, enabling it to take some of the most able boys. UCS absorbed all these changes, offering a curriculum with a breadth that might have astonished some of Slaughter's predecessors, and sustained an overall excellence in the quality of teaching. As director of studies, Peter Underwood helped to introduce a timetable based around the choices made by boys, enabling them to have as wide a choice of subjects as possible, at both GCSE and A level. This system continued as a key academic feature under his successor John Older, who noted that it was 'very much in the UCS tradition of allowing individuality to be the predominant factor'. The combined result of all this was that by 1996 almost every boy was securing passes in every public examination he sat; every GCSE candidate was achieving six C grades or above, 80 per cent of boys were gaining A and B grades at A level, and nearly every sixth-former left UCS with a place on a degree course, with around thirty of them going to Oxbridge. These results were gained without diluting in any way the essential humanity of the school's ethos, in that UCS never refused to take anyone from the lowest achievers at GCSE if they were committed to studying for A levels.

Part of this success came because Council at UCS, encouraged by Giles Slaughter, finally started to invest in new learning and sporting facilities at Frognal. Slaughter recognised that this was an area where UCS was lagging behind other schools. His paper, *Towards 2000*, prepared in 1985, provided much-needed impetus towards the planning of overdue developments. The paper not only encompassed physical improvements, but also considered issues such as the school's location, co-education and the creation of a pre-prep school. The building plans were revealed to the school during 1986. They envisaged a purpose-built sports hall and the transformation of the existing gym into classrooms, freeing up space for the creation of a new and more fitting library, the old one being converted into more laboratories. The idea of relocating the whole school was discounted, both then and a little later on. As far as the admission of girls was concerned, there was agreement in principle that they should be permitted to enter only the sixth form, although it was regarded as unlikely that this would happen before the mid-1990s at least.

It was to be several years later, and following two more papers from the head, before serious work began on translating his vision into reality. Partly this was because of the way in which Council was structured, hindering practical progress; there was little integration between the teaching and the financial and administrative sides of the school, which made the delivery of any vision difficult. Delays also occurred because the question of how these ambitions would be financed was never satisfactorily scrutinised. So although planning consent for a sports hall was received in 1989, it was impossible for the school to proceed through lack of funds. The initial solution was based on relocating the Junior Branch to new premises built on land owned by UCS at West Hampstead, disposing of the valuable Holly Hill site and selling part of the West Hampstead land for housing. But the development proposals incurred local opposition and the scheme was withdrawn. By the spring of 1991 progress had been slow and there were suggestions that poor facilities were starting to cause recruitment problems. The head reported to Council that 'we simply do not have enough to put on show'. The development programme could no longer be delayed.

A development subcommittee was formed under the chairmanship of Sir Colin Marshall, later Lord Marshall, much of the work in bringing plans to fruition being done by the head in association with three Council members, Alan Greengross, Tony Hillier and Ian King. A valuable role was also played by fellow members John Slack, Council chairman from 1980 until 1987, Geoffrey Maitland Smith, his successor from 1987 to 1994, and John Waddington, the treasurer. It was clear that the only way forward to pay for development was by increasing income through recruiting more pupils. The solution was to begin admitting boys to the Junior Branch at the age of seven, creating the space to do so by sending boys from Holly Hill to Frognal at the age of eleven. Overall numbers would rise from 784 to 920. This would not only help to fund the immediate plans for Frognal, but would generally strengthen the school's finances in the process.

There had already been some physical improvements at Holly Hill, but Ian McGregor had been making a persuasive case for further development. McGregor retired just as plans were being finalised in 1991. Described as 'a man who respected the individual characteristics in every boy … a man of expansive wit, great culture, humour, intellect and, above all, gentleness with staff, parents and boys', he had brought the Junior Branch into the modern educational era. As was traditional, his successor, John Hubbard, was drawn from the ranks of the UCS common room. Hubbard had given considerable service to UCS as head of chemistry, head of science, Deme warden of

Top: Geoffrey Maitland Smith, Council Chairman, Giles Slaughter and Peter Jay, Guest of Honour at prize-giving, 1995.

Above: Ian McGregor retired as head of the Junior Branch in 1991. He respected the individuality of every boy and is remembered fondly for his wisdom, sense of humour and gentleness.

Below: John Hubbard took over as headmaster of the Junior Branch in 1991 until his retirement in 2001.

Sports Day.

BELOW: Library.

BOTTOM: Studying in the Giles Slaughter Wing.

Flooks, sixth-form tutor and games coach. He would serve as head of the Junior Branch until 2001, leading it through a period of considerable transformation. This not only encompassed the changes being proposed in relation to the age range within the school and the physical improvements that were planned, but also the external changes affecting the primary curriculum. During this time Hubbard particularly appreciated the advice and support given by Colin Holloway. A former pupil, member of staff, Deme warden and third master, who had been appointed to Council in 1997, Holloway had left UCS to become head of the junior school at King's College School, and this experience was to prove invaluable, not only to John Hubbard, but also to Council.

When Hubbard took up the headship of the Junior Branch, it was not the job he had envisaged. At the time, the proposals were still to build a new school, on a new site, for eight- to thirteen-year-olds. The subsequent changes, which were agreed before informing the Junior Branch staff, made the post he took up very different from the one he had accepted. As a result, he would recommend that in future the Junior Branch headship should be openly advertised, and that his successor should have experience and training in the primary sector. Nevertheless, it was widely agreed that Hubbard carried out a difficult task very well.

At UCS, admitting boys at the age of eleven had a fundamental but beneficial impact on the school. Previously teaching had been focused almost entirely on public examinations, when only a single year between the ages of thirteen and eighteen did not involve an examination of some sort. The new arrangements freed staff to concentrate on meeting the educational needs of eleven-year-olds. Among the consequences of this was the increasing importance of personal, social and health education (PSHE) in the lower school, again in keeping with the school tradition of developing each pupil as an individual. The form for the new entry was named Shell – the headmaster later admitted he drew his inspiration from Billy Bunter (which, of course, had links with UCS in any case through the actor Gerald Campion).

Alongside these changes, the school also launched a development appeal in July 1993, under the direction of Frances Isaacs. By then the first phase of the redevelopment had finally begun. This featured the creation of a new library (which would be named after the Enav family in thanks for their generous donation); an East Wing (later named the Giles Slaughter Wing), consisting of a music school, computer laboratory, lecture theatre and suite of maths classrooms; and the redevelopment of the crypt (the level of the playground having been lowered to let in more light), with new classrooms, a history library, fitness studio and darkroom. To achieve all this the old gyms had to be removed, so a temporary sports hall was constructed on the site of

Senior School Staff 1997. Back row, from left: Allan Steven, Richard Welch, Mike Lewis, Mike McElroy, Russell Chapman, Michael Howat, Geoffrey Plow, Adrian McManus, Nigel Peace, Jeremy Hudson, Chris Mahon, Jeff Edwards, David Woodhead, Jeremy Fox, Andrew Boulton, Agnes Ope, Susan Taylor, Lucy Magala, Margaret Amanze, Dave Mullins, Johnny Bass, Ciro Tufano, Sallah Eddine Khifli. Fourth row: Stan Rynkowski, Rory Bolger, Stewart Fitzgerald, Andy Davis, Paul Ellis, Gareth Lewis, John Bradbury, Jack Watson, Simon Bloomfield, Neil McNaughton, Michael Walsh, Peter Hopkins, Colin Myles, Dave Chapman, Kevin Reilly, Michael Kelly, Sonny Velupillay, John Boal, Jo Eggleton, Terry Morris. Third Row: Laurence Tiger, Paul Eggleton, Adrian McAra, Roy Hyde, Tony Gowlett, Mook Matuszak, Roland Hawkins, Andrew Haggar, Geoffrey Greenhough, David Rance, Daniel Cross, Steve Wells, Casimir Bowes Jones, Tony Roberts, Martin Hitchcock, Hugh de Camillis, Carol Goldblatt, Diana Meynell. Second row: Andrew Wilkes, Rodney Mellor, Tom Youlden, Keith Garwood, Steven Hann, Martin Smith, Patricia Karet, Barry Bateman, Ian Cornish, Mike Alsford, David Lund, Steve Jacobi, Allan Woolley, David Colwell, Mike Collins, Julia Aspinall, Sue St John, Naomi Greenwood, Enda Curran. Front Row: Ruth Beedle, Sue Lobatto, Thanh Kent, Margie Daniel, Janet Rofail, Andrea Bollons, Gill Heywood, Karen Hudson, Peter and Margaret Underwood, Kenneth and Vivienne Durham, John Older, Maria Dunn, Alison Nolan-Cain, Hazel Eggleton, Geneviève Mori, Anne Isaac.

the shale tennis courts at the rear of the school. Plans were being finalised for a more space-efficient version of the originally planned sports hall, which was scheduled for construction in the late 1990s. Work began on the East Wing in the spring of 1994 and by the following August the new library, additional laboratories and more classrooms were also complete. During the summer of 1995, as work on this phase of development drew to a close, the appeal reached its target of a million pounds.

Giles Slaughter retired in 1996. He left a school where he had been deeply happy. He himself felt that it was a more efficient school, a school with a greater sense of urgency. In almost every aspect of school life there had been improvements. But he also had no doubt, as he had noted at speech day ten years before, that the principles set down by the founders of the school in 1830 remained just as relevant as UCS approached the twenty-first century: 'the pursuit of academic excellence, a respect for and the encouragement of independent thought and individual judgement in the general setting of toleration and regard for one another's beliefs'.

7

'A living article of faith'
1996 onwards

'Another friendly, confident man with a passion for UCS' was how the school captain described the school's new headmaster. Kenneth Durham came to UCS from King's College School, Wimbledon, UCS's traditional rival, where he had been director of studies. Previously he had been at St Albans School for twelve years, where he was head of economics. Educated at St John's, Leatherhead, he had read philosophy, politics and economics at Brasenose, Oxford. Durham, in his early forties, had never visited the school before applying for the post, but found on his appointment that UCS, combining an academic education in an unstuffy way with a liberal environment, could not have suited him better. It was, he says, 'an extraordinarily happy accident'.

World Cup fever, 2002.

Kenneth Durham took over as Headmaster in 1996.

BELOW: In 1999 a new Deme was created, named after Peter Underwood who retired in 1997 after 36 years' service.

BOTTOM: Sir Victor Blank became chairman of the Council in 1995.

Durham was the right man at the right time. It was not that there was much to do in terms of physical development in the first instance. But by the late 1990s, as the school magazine put it, the educational world had become 'increasingly dominated by a national curriculum, by schemes of work, by modular examinations and by "key skills"'. It was no longer enough for teaching to be a matter of personality and charisma. Durham's predecessor saw that and, not liking what he saw, knew it was time to hand over the reins.

Initially the new headmaster had enough to do in managing the consequences of the admission of pupils to UCS at eleven. New relationships were being forged with feeder schools. Year groups and staff were being adjusted and new appointments made. In September 1999, to cope with increased numbers, a fifth Deme was created, named Underwoods after Peter Underwood, who had retired two years before as vice-master after thirty-six years on the staff. Described as 'this smiling, forthright Cornishman', Underwood had been a vibrant presence in the common room and throughout the school. His successor was John Older, kind, sensitive, appreciative and humorous, who served until his own retirement in 2004.

Alongside this came the managerial changes needed for UCS to keep pace with the changing educational environment. The weekly meetings instituted by Walton still remained the basis for running the school, but the team had expanded to a degree which made it too unwieldy to be effective. Moreover, it had no strategic remit, but concentrated instead on more immediate pastoral and organisational matters. Durham streamlined school management, making it more positive and responsive. This came about gradually and sensitively to avoid the immediate reaction Durham found to change in the school, which was to question whether it could possibly be any improvement over 'the UCS way'. In creating a senior management team, with only seven members, one of whom was a deputy head charged with responsibility for pastoral care, Durham had to overcome the feeling that this was a challenge to the autonomy of the Deme wardens. This concern was overstated: the Demes are still a fundamental part of school life. At the same time, the head set about bringing the practice of the school into line with modern educational requirements, putting in place the relevant written policies, while ensuring that the underlying liberal characteristics of the school remained intact.

Alongside the reforms being made by the head were changes to the way in which Council operated. Sir Victor Blank had assumed the chairmanship in 1995. He and several of his colleagues believed that Council needed to become a much more effective strategic body. The new head appreciated the drive of his chairman in supporting his vision for the school and in galvanising the Council to take on ambitious projects.

Durham did not believe in change for change's sake. He continued the policy of broadening the school curriculum and allowing boys considerable freedom in their choice of subjects, which could be seen as the modern, more efficient version of Key's original scheme. Key would have applauded the inclusion of subjects such as philosophy and geology, but may have been mystified by the introduction of remote learning opportunities through the use of computer technology. He would also have appreciated the battle, still persisting in the twenty-first century, to strike a balance in teaching between the needs of the individual pupil and the requirements of the examination system. Given the glowing report that teaching at UCS received after the inspection conducted in 2005, it is hardly surprising that the school's academic progress has been maintained. Almost all boys were achieving at least a grade C in every GCSE subject, with over 80 per cent achieving either A or A*. At A level, A and B grades were awarded to more than 90 per cent of boys, enabling a similar percentage to gain their first-choice university place.

Another trend has been the creation of an even wider range of recreational opportunities for boys. There are impressive opportunities in drama, art and music. The school forged new musical partnerships with other

The Headmaster chats to pupils in his study.

The school continues its long tradition of excellence in the arts. BELOW, CLOCKWISE FROM TOP LEFT: band playing in the great hall; *Our Country's Good*, 2005; working in the art room; *The Tempest* by 6E, 2002; piano practice.

schools at home and abroad, holding joint concerts with the London Oratory and the Gymnasium Corvinianum from Northeim in Germany. An innovative annual book festival was established, bringing literary stars such as Carol Ann Duffy, Andrew Motion and John Le Carré to the school, while the new poetry society was named the Gunn Club after an illustrious Old Gower. Boys seem to travel to every corner of the world, whether to Cornwall on an investigation into rural deprivation, to Germany and France on exchange visits, to Uganda to help in Robert Kamasaka's Equatorial College School, to South Africa on a rugby tour or to Australia on a geography expedition. The school's inclusive sporting philosophy allows boys with enthusiasm and commitment to appear in school teams, while internal competitions, including a revived sports day, provide plenty of opportunities for entertaining rivalry. Speech days were pepped up by the ability of the Council chairman, Sir Victor Blank, to attract a stream of appealing speakers, from rugby star Michael Lynagh and former international footballer Gary Lineker, to impressionist Rory Bremner and polymath Stephen Fry.

The activities on offer at Frognal were mirrored by those available at the Junior Branch, from which UCS still receives nearly three-quarters of its entrants. Here facilities had also been improved, featuring new teaching blocks, a drama studio and a larger library. In 2001 John Hubbard handed on Bunny Lake's 'hasta sacra' to his successor, Kevin Douglas, the first outsider recruited to head the JB. The Governers were keen to appoint a junior specialist and Douglas had come from ten years as deputy head of Belmont,

BELOW FROM LEFT: Gary Lineker distributing prizes, 2004; performance poet Adisa during Book Week; a new poetry group was named after the poet, Thom Gunn, who was a pupil at the School.

Junior boys in the library.

Mill Hill's Preparatory School. But Charles Simmons and those who followed him would recognise in Douglas a like-minded commitment to the principles embodied in the Junior Branch, a commitment also recognised by the school inspectors in 2005. Douglas was himself a former ISI school inspector. Having trained at Loughborough University and played rugby for Harlequins, Saracens and England U-23, he was attracted to UCS by its ethos, academic reputation and belief in the broad curriculum. 'Teaching,' he noted in 2005, 'is about turning out well-rounded and happy pupils.'

The idea of establishing a pre-prep school for pupils under the age of seven finally materialised in 2002. Rather than create an entirely new school, Council decided that it would be more effective to acquire an existing school. The Phoenix School, in nearby College Crescent, a co-educational nursery and pre-prep school, became part of UCS in December 2002. Under Kevin Douglas and Jane Humble, the first head of The Phoenix, integration was achieved very smoothly. This also marked the establishment of the UCS Foundation, completing the evolution of the school from the department of

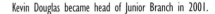

Kevin Douglas became head of Junior Branch in 2001.

ABOVE: The Phoenix, a co-educational pre-prep, became part of UCS in 2002.

BELOW: Jane Humble, first head of The Phoenix.

BOTTOM: Lisa Mason-Jones was appointed in 2007.

another institution, University College, into a free-standing school and, ultimately, an independent educational foundation.

With a catchment area comprising essentially Hampstead, Hampstead Garden Suburb, Hendon, Finchley, Islington and St John's Wood, UCS remains a largely local school, but with a much more ethnically diverse population than in the past. This has obvious advantages for both the school and the boys, since it makes UCS a focus for strong local friendships. The traditional absence of religious affiliations and Saturday morning classes, plus the cultural diversity of the modern school, still attracts the sons of local Jewish families to UCS. In recent years the school has been strengthening its local links not just with primary schools in the area, but also through a more active participation by boys in community work, although fund-raising remains the central way UCS contributes towards charitable projects, raising the remarkable sum of £44,000 in 2005 through a broad range of different events.

The head has placed considerable emphasis on the role of the school in the community, and turning the school to look outwards has been one of his key aims. This is being achieved not only through international links with other schools, whether in Europe or Africa, or through links with other similar schools, but also through developing stronger relationships with community organisations and using the school's strengths to develop new partnerships. One notable example has been the educational partnership between the geography departments of UCS and Sir James Smith's School in Camelford in Cornwall, where staff and pupils work together in the field and share information. Other activities have involved boys working in local primary schools, helping in charity shops, organising an annual dinner for elderly people and assisting local disabled children.

The obligation on the school to expand its community involvement was an integral part of the five-year plan drawn up to take UCS through to 2008–09. An allied part of that aim, harking back to the days when scholarship boys from local authorities were such a distinctive part of the school, was to broaden the school's intake. The development of a significant bursary fund will provide financial support for eighty boys. In moving the school forward, the plan also envisaged further physical improvements, completing the plans originally set out ten years earlier and investing in further expansion. As the head emphasised to parents, 'the process of improvement must be never-ending'. Work began on the long-planned sports hall in 2004 and the new state-of-the-art centre, incorporating a 25-metre heated pool, was completed in 2006. In preparation for the admission of girls, sixth-form accommodation will be extended and improved. Further investment will be made in teaching facilities (making use of the latest in computer technology), in internal recreation space and in facilities for the school administration. In support of

Junior rugby.

A passion for percussion – members of the Junior Branch playing the glockenspiel.

these proposals, an appeal was launched late in 2005 to raise £2 million by 2007, marking the centenary of the school's relocation to Hampstead. The ambition of the proposed expansion plans is reflected in their total estimated cost of some £15 million.

The headmaster also wanted the future development of the school to underscore the distinctive qualities fundamental to its progress since its foundation. Although the school is free from religious affiliations, it is, noted an inspection report in 1999, 'composed of many types of spirituality and is imbued with a high moral sense'. Several faith societies are run by boys, while assemblies provide an opportunity to send out moral messages. Kenneth Durham, like so many of his predecessors, has recognised that the essentially liberal nature of the school depends on self-discipline as well as freedom. So intellectual curiosity, breadth of study and independence of mind must continue to be an integral part of, and never subordinate to, academic excellence. If that is to be the case, the school should continue to make sure, wrote the head, echoing so many of his predecessors, that the curriculum 'is stimulating and broad rather than simply offering preparation for examinations'. Nor should there be any complacency about the openness and tolerance on which the strength of the school's pastoral care is based. This

ABOVE LEFT: Old Gowers at Corporation Centenary Dinner at the School, 2005. RIGHT: The headmaster at the dinner.

Listening to a lecture.

careful balance has proved in UCS that a plethora of rules governing behaviour and appearance, a fashionable tool for driving up standards in many schools, is unnecessary for the creation and maintenance of a civilised society. UCS works, as it always has, not through systems and structures, but through relationships.

Those on the outside still puzzle over this. School inspectors, in the course of an outstanding report on UCS in 2005, were plainly mystified by the freedom that only occasionally encouraged boys to overstep the mark, that brought a dilatoriness in moving between lessons, that allowed them to dress in a combination of blazer, unbuttoned shirt, scruffy trousers and trainers. (One inspector, noticing a dress-down day was shortly to be held, asked the member of staff who was with him how they could tell the difference from an ordinary school day.) They were mystified because, in spite of or because of this, boys at UCS remain friendly and courteous, articulate and confident, tolerant and respectful of others. They were, wrote the inspectors in 1999, 'sparkling' in their nonconformity.

This ethos is based on a partnership between all those involved within the school, from the headmaster downwards. The importance of long-serving staff in fostering this from one generation of boys to another cannot be underestimated. But younger staff, newly appointed to the school, while absorbing the atmosphere within UCS, also play an invaluable part in their enthusiasm for change and the introduction of new ideas, an essential part of the motor of progress.

As the school celebrates one hundred years at Hampstead, the Centennial Development Plan encompasses new initiatives intended not only to consolidate key elements of UCS's ethos, but also to take the school forward in the same spirit. The proposed bursary fund hopes to play a part in bringing about the happy mix of ability, social and ethnic backgrounds for which many previous heads have striven. The introduction of girls to the sixth form will advance this inclusivity in the realisation of an idea first talked about in the 1960s, and some would say long overdue for implementation. Plans for a new art, design and modern languages facility will maintain the school's tradition of a broad curriculum and a commitment to fostering the aptitude of all students. The entire plan, particularly the creation of a permanent development office and a revenue-raising sports club, aims to secure the financial security which eluded the school for much of its history.

Past traditions, present accomplishments and future plans all form part of what Kenneth Durham has described as 'a living article of faith'. It is remarkable how constant the school has been over nearly two centuries in sustaining the founding ethos. It is worth repeating the words already quoted from Thomas Key – his belief that for each pupil to follow

Jubilee picnic, 2002.

a liberal profession, it is absolutely necessary in order that he may manfully succeed to his own satisfaction, that he shall be able to clear away all prejudice, and to gauge and weigh the men he meets by their own individual merit, whatever their parentage may be and whatever their set may be.

From this philosophy springs much of what makes up UCS. The breadth of choice in the curriculum and in extra-curricular activities not only gives all students the chance to find a niche for the development of their own talents, but also provides them with as broad a horizon as possible against which to form their own judgements about the world around them. Key regarded as central in all this the relationship between each student and his peers, and between pupils and staff. Every one of his successors, in their varied ways, has continued to subscribe to this approach. This, in Eve's phrase, has produced the school's 'sweet reasonableness', that unique combination of openness, freedom, tolerance, vitality and responsibility, the success of which has foxed so many outsiders. Today the UCS ethos remains as it ever has, in the words of the headmaster:

Working together.

the belief in a broad, open, tolerant community, with a commitment to the development of the individual student through intellectual stimulation, through breadth of opportunity, through culture and through compassion.

List of Subscribers

JOHN TREVOR ADAMS 1948–54, UCS
MALCOLM ALEXANDER 1956–62, UCS
OMAR MOWLA ALI 2005– , UCS
ADAM AND KARIM AMIJEE ALIBHAI
    1994–2007, UCS
JOHN ALLEN 1946–52, UCS
A R TONY AMOR 1956–63, UCS
IFOR AP GLYN 1972–1979, UCS
ELLIOT ARWAS 1990–2000, UCS
KENNETH AYLMER 1956–61, UCS
PROFESSOR ADAM BALEN 1968–78, UCS
SIR ROGER BANNISTER 1944–46, governor,
    parent and UCS
C D BARNARD 1941–48, UCS
JAYNE AND ALISTAIR BARR 2004– , parents
IAN BARR 1991– , parent and member of staff
IANN BARRON 1947–55, UCS and governor
STEPHEN THOMAS BEACH 1949–59, UCS
C C C BEALES 1958–67, UCS
SAM BEECHAM 2000– , UCS
MAX BEECHAM 2004– , UCS
TERENCE P BEEDLE 1956–64, UCS
CAROL BEETLES 1999–2006, parent
DAVID AND PETER BERNARD 1977–85,
    UCS
ZUBER & ZORAVAR BISHNOI 2000– , UCS
ELLIOTT BOGERT 2003– , UCS
W L BOOTH 1936–45, UCS
JOHN BRADBURY 1990–, member of staff
RICHARD BRADLEY1943–52, UCS
BRIAN BRAUNS 1949–53, UCS
R A BRIDE 1935–42, UCS
ANDREW BRIDGWATER 1953–65, UCS
HENRY BRITTAIN 2005– , UCS
BEN BROOKS 2003– , UCS
MICHAEL BRUNNER 1976–81, UCS
ANDREW R BRYSON 1952–61, UCS
W J BUCKLAND 1938–48, UCS
DR DEREK BUNN former school doctor, 1977–99
CJ BURKE 2005– , UCS
ALEXANDER EDWARD BURTON 1993–2002,
    UCS
WENDY BURTON 2003– , parent
STEPHEN BUSS 1954–61, UCS
JEFFREY H CALVERT 1962–72, UCS
PAUL CARTON 1966–71, UCS
MICHAEL CARTWRIGHT 1960–66, UCS
ALEXANDER CEDAR 2004– , UCS
GARETH CHAN 1997–2007, UCS
BENJAMIN, TIMOTHY AND SAM CHURCHILL
COLIN CLARK 1943–53, UCS

ROBIN CLARK 1945–55, UCS
M JOHN CLAYTON 1951–55, UCS
JOSHUA AND GIDEON COHEN 2005–,
    UCS
EDEN CONFINO 2005– , UCS
PETER F T CORBETT 1942–49, UCS
GEOFFREY CORNWALL 1953–64, UCS
G MARTIN COURTIER 1949–57, UCS
BENEDICT CRAVEN1997–, UCS
DENNIS E CREASY 1943–49, UCS
DR ADRIAN CRISP 1962–66, UCS
PETER CRUTTWELL 1947–56, UCS
NICHOLAS P CUTCLIFFE 1930–37, UCS
OLIVER DAVIS 2005– , UCS
M G DELAHOOKE 1944–53
J MALCOLM DENNES 1959–64, UCS
DAVID DESAI 1999– , UCS
A J DREW 1943–50, UCS
D G DRIVER 1949–55, UCS
HOWARD DRURY 1943–1952, UCS
MARTIN DULCKEN 1943–54, UCS
JOHN G DUNBAR 1943–48, UCS
ALEXANDER DWEK 1996–2006, UCS
EDEN DWEK 1998– , UCS
JOSH EILON 2002– , UCS
ROBERT A ELRICK 1947–53, UCS
CHRIS ELSTON 1949–57, UCS
MRS B EMANUEL 1998– , parent
MICHAEL EVANS 1945–51, UCS
DR NORMAN EVE 1939–44, UCS
MICHAEL A FALTER 1959–67, UCS
ED FENWICK 2002–07, UCS
MICHAEL FIDLER 1978–88, UCS
DAVID FISHER 1962–67, UCS
DAVEED D FLANDERS 1965–66, UCS
HUGO FLETCHER 1945–52, UCS
JOHN R FOOTTIT 1941–44, UCS
STEPHEN FORSTER 1948–58, UCS
WILLIAM JONATHAN FORSTER 1957–65,
    UCS
CHRISTOPHER FOX UCS 1999– ,
M A O FOX 1956–65, UCS
JOSHUA FRASER 2003– , UCS
JONATHAN MD FREEDMAN 1994–99, UCS
DAN FRIEDBERG 1978–80, UCS
HENRY FUZ-KEEVE 2003–06, UCS
MATTHEW GOLD 2000– , UCS
DR JON GOLDIN 1974–84, UCS
DANIEL GOLDSTEIN 2004– , UCS
JOSHUA GOODMAN 2005– , UCS
ELLIOT GORDON 2005– , UCS

JOSHUA GOTTLIEB 1997– , UCS
ADAM GOULD 2002–2007, UCS
CHARLIE AND JAMES GOULD 2000– , UCS
SAM AND JOEY GREENBERG 2006– , UCS
JOHN G GROVES 1952–62, UCS
KENNETH HAGUE 1945–51, UCS
JOHN C HALL 1952–57, UCS
ANTHONY P HAMMOND 1960–65, UCS
SAM HELFGOTT 2004– , UCS
A E HENRY 1934–37, UCS
JAKE HERMAN 2006– , UCS
M A HETHERINGTON 1946–53, UCS
J G HEWETT 1944–54, UCS
DR M S HIGGS 1948–52, UCS
C MALCOLM M HOBDELL 1950–61, UCS
DAVID HOFFMAN 1989–2000, UCS
DAVID HOLDER 1950–59, UCS
JULIAN HOLDER 1976–83, UCS
COLIN HOLLOWAY 1946–55, UCS; 1959–76,
    staff; 1997– , governor
RICHARD HOLMES 1968–78, UCS
GARRY G HORNE 1945–55, UCS
MR MICHAEL HOWE 1947–54, UCS
JOHN HUBBARD 1966–2001, staff
BERNARD J HUMPHREY 1953–60; UCS
DAVID HUNT 1963–69, UCS
MR PHILIP R W HUNT 1967–76, UCS
ANDREW HYMAN 1986–93, UCS
JOE HYTNER 2001–06, UCS
R N JACKSON 1937–41, UCS
MATTHEW JACOBS 1994–2005, UCS
MARK JESNICK 1996–2007, UCS
M J JONES 1944–50, UCS
JONATHAN KANTER 1977–88, UCS
DAVID KEATING 1954–61, UCS
MICHAEL KETTIROS 1995–2003, UCS
AMIR KHOYLOU 2000– , UCS
IAN C KING 1943–52, UCS
BEN H KNIGHTS 1931–36, UCS
PAUL KRIKLER 1969–1979, UCS
EDWIN KROPMAN 2006– , UCS
GRAEME WENTWORTH KYLE 1948–59, UCS
TOM LAKE 1996–2003, UCS
JONATHAN LAU 1998– , UCS
DAVID LAWRENCE 2000–07, UCS
MATTHEW LEACH 1975–86, UCS
G LEDERER 1940–45, UCS
BEN LEDSOM 1997– , UCS
DOMINIC LEVENE 2005– , UCS
ADAM P LEVINE 1997–2007, UCS
JOSHUA M LEVINE 1994–2005, UCS

PETER LIDDELOW 1944–50, UCS

A C LITTLE 1933–1940, UCS

TIMOTHY, FRANCIS and CHRISTOPHER LOCKIE 1985–98, UCS

DR D R LUCAS 1932–40, UCS

G F LYFORD 1940–44, UCS

D C MABBETT 1933–40, UCS

DAVID MACLEAN WATT 2002– , Governor

JOHN MACLENNAN 1958–67, UCS

BEN MAIER 2000–06, UCS

GEOFFREY MAITLAND SMITH 1987–96, UCS, Governor and Chairman of Council

ANDREW MALLESON 1949–60, UCS

LORD MARSHALL OF KNIGHTSBRIDGE 1946–51, UCS

JOHN DOUGLAS MARSHALL 1950–85, Rev. parent; staff

DANIEL MATLIN 1994–2000, UCS

MARK MCANERNEY 2005– , UCS

ADRIAN MCBRIDE 2002– , UCS

JOHN BRIAN MCKEE 1954–58, UCS

MAX BRIDGES MCMAHON 2006– , UCS

ANTHONY RICHARD MILLARD 1947–51, UCS

SVILEN MIRTCHEV 2001– , UCS

JOHN STANLEY MOPPETT 1942–48, UCS

TERRY MORRIS 1970– , staff; parent

R H MURDOCH 1927–32, UCS

G NADIN 1924–34, UCS

PATRICK NAYLOR 1942–52, parent; UCS

SAUL and JOAL NELSON

GEORGE ANTHONY OFFORD 1954–60, UCS

DANIEL OKIN 1994–2005, UCS

WILLIAM ORCHARD 2005– , UCS

PAUL OSPALAK 1939–44, UCS

ROGER J OUSTON 1946–1956, UCS

JOSEPH PARIS 2002– ,UCS

STEPHEN M PARKHURST 1947–56, UCS

C J PARRY 1947–53, UCS

CATO PASTOLL 2005– , UCS

DR MARTIN PAYNE 1964–71, UCS

DOMINIC F PINTO 1964–73, UCS

DR GEOFFREY PLOW, 1982– Staff member

MR and MRS COS PRATSIDES, 1995 –2005 parents

W J PRICE 1945–52, UCS

ANTHONY PRITCHARD 1950–58, UCS

ANDREW PULVER 1974–84, UCS

J QUICK 1936–42, UCS; Member of Council

DAVID P RANCE 1962–69, UCS; 1979–, Staff Member

NEIL REES 1944–47, UCS

HIS HONOUR MARTIN REYNOLDS 1945–55, UCS

TOM RICHARD 1933–41, UCS

OSCAR RIGG 2006–, UCS

DANIEL ROFAIL 2003– , UCS

C R T ROWE 1943–51, UCS

JOHN LITTLEJOHN ROBBINS 1924–28, UCS

JOHN D ROWEN 1957–61, UCS

THE VERY REVEREND MICHAEL SADGROVE 1959–67, UCS

JOSH AND ALEX SAXBY UCS 1996–, UCS

SOL AND SAMUEL SCHLAGMAN 2004– , UCS

BENJAMIN SCHWARZ 1998–2005, UCS

DANIEL SCHWARZ 2000–07, UCS

R H SCOPES 1952–62, UCS

MRS J A SCOTT 2002– , Staff member

DECLAN SELBO 2002– , UCS

ANTHONY SHARP 1973–80, UCS

DANIEL and ROBERT SHER 2000– , UCS

ANDREW C SIMPSON 1967–74, UCS

GILES SLAUGHTER 1983–96, Headmaster

PROF SIMON A SMAIL, CBE 1958–64, UCS

ELLIOTT SMITH 2003– , UCS

SAMUEL SMITH 2001– , UCS

ZAKARI SMITH 2001– , UCS

DR N J C SNELL 1960–66, UCS

ERNST SONDHEIMER 1937–41, UCS

DAVID SOULSBY 1949–56, UCS

JAMES D K SOUTHON 2004– , UCS

JOHN STAPLES 1953–62, UCS

MARCUS STEVENSON 2006– , UCS

ADAM SUISSA 1995–2004, UCS

JOEL SUISSA 1997– , UCS

VELUPILLAY SURESAN 1988– , Staff member

DONALD THOMAS SWIFT-HOOK 1943–50, UCS

MR and MRS R TAGGART 2003– , parents

MATHEW TATA 1998–2007, UCS

NEIL TAYLOR 1959–66, UCS

ANTHONY THOMPSON 1947–56, UCS

IAIN THOMPSON 2004– , UCS

MALCOLM THORNDIKE 1943–51, UCS

CHRISTIAN TOMASZEWSKI 2003– , UCS

PAUL TURNER 1949–60, UCS

RONALD E ULMANN 1945–52, UCS

HEMANT VASWANI 2006– , UCS

CHARLES WADE 1998– , UCS

D P WADE 1932–39, UCS

JOE WADSWORTH 2006– , UCS

MALCOLM J H WAKE 1945–56, UCS

REX WALFORD 1945–52, UCS

DAVID WALLACE 1969–74, UCS

DAVID WATERMAN 1979–89, UCS

MARC WATERMAN 1978–85, UCS

JOHN C WATSON 1951–61, UCS

TOBY WEINBERG 2002– , UCS

THEODORE WEISS 2002–, UCS

CHRISTOPHER J S WELCH 1961–70, UCS

ALAN WEST 1994–2001, UCS

BRIAN R WHITBY 1951–58,UCS

MICHAEL WIEDER 1997–2002, UCS

P W WIGLEY 1951–61, UCS

JULIAN WILLIAMS 2002–2007, UCS

ADAM WILLMAN 1993–2000, UCS

DAVID WILLMAN 1988–1995, UCS

J A C WILSON 1933–36, UCS

ROBIN WILSON 1952–62, UCS

JEDD WISE 2005– , UCS

JONATHAN WISEMAN 1988–1998, UCS

A M J WOOD 1949–57, UCS

GREGORY WOODCOCK 2001–06, UCS

MARTIN WRIGHT 1982–89, UCS

DAVID YORATH 1957–64, UCS

RYAN K ZAMAN 2004– , UCS

Index